DECADES

Mott The Hoople
& Ian Hunter
in the 1970s

John Van der Kiste

sonicbondpublishing.com

Sonicbond Publishing Limited
www.sonicbondpublishing.co.uk
Email: info@sonicbondpublishing.co.uk

First Published in the United Kingdom 2022
First Published in the United States 2022

British Library Cataloguing in Publication Data:
A Catalogue record for this book is available from the British Library

Copyright John Van der Kiste 2022

ISBN 978-1-78952-162-7

Typeset in ITC Garamond & ITC Avant Garde
Printed and bound in England

Graphic design and typesetting: Full Moon Media

Foreword

At the start of the 1970s – to those of us who bought the music papers each week or shared someone else's and looked through friends' record collections with an almost obsessional interest – few British acts seemed to exert a more powerful mystique than Mott The Hoople. The media categorised them as 'an albums band', and with three failed singles to their name – rarely played on the radio – few of us knew what they really sounded like. Their radio sessions were a rarity, and LPs were something we diligently saved up for: not bought on spec. But the inkies' coverage of the band suggested that they were something special.

Two years later, they were daytime radio favourites and *Top of the Pops* regulars. Their period at the summit of the fickle music business was short but glorious. Over half a century has elapsed since their first album, but the recorded music of Ian Hunter, Mott The Hoople and *the Hoople family* still sounds as powerful and enigmatic as it ever did. The 1970s were a bewildering decade for them – a Switchback Railway of highs and lows.

Anybody studying the work of the group, its offshoots and the music of its frontman Ian Hunter, cannot but acknowledge several years of painstaking work by Campbell Devine – author of the group's first major biography and, more recently, two full volumes on the life and work of Ian Hunter, and many of the comprehensive booklet notes accompanying their recent CD reissues. All Devine's writings are based on years of following the group and their subsequent offshoots and careers, interviewing several members, other musicians, producers and those who knew them: some sadly no longer with us. I would like to place on record my gratitude for his work, and also thank Adrian Perkins, who has run the excellent Mott The Hoople website – a mine of information – for many years; Kev Hunter (no relation), who helped supply many of the images; Gus Goad and Russ Ballard, who generously shared with me information on various aspects of the whole saga, and my rock-friend of many years' standing, Miles Tredinnick, for his thoughts and ever-helpful emails in which we discussed a group he has likewise loved for years. I am also indebted to my wife Kim, who has, as ever, been an unfailing support during my writing and research. And last but not least, thanks to my ever-supportive publisher Stephen Lambe and the Sonicbond editorial team.

Would you like to write for Sonicbond Publishing?

At Sonicbond Publishing we are always on the look-out for authors, particularly for our two main series:

On Track. Mixing fact with in depth analysis, the On Track series examines the work of a particular musical artist or group. All genres are considered from easy listening and jazz to 60s soul to 90s pop, via rock and metal.

On Screen. This series looks at the world of film and television. Subjects considered include directors, actors and writers, as well as entire television and film series. As with the On Track series, we balance fact with analysis.

While professional writing experience would, of course, be an advantage the most important qualification is to have real enthusiasm and knowledge of your subject. First-time authors are welcomed, but the ability to write well in English is essential.

Sonicbond Publishing has distribution throughout Europe and North America, and all books are also published in E-book form. Authors will be paid a royalty based on sales of their book.

Further details are available from www.sonicbondpublishing. co.uk. To contact us, complete the contact form there or email info@sonicbondpublishing.co.uk

DECADES | Mott The Hoople & Ian Hunter in the 1970s

Contents

Introduction

In the early-1960s, a generation of British youngsters – mostly in their
mid-teens and generally still at school – were forming their own skiffle
or beat groups. While the Hereford area could never claim to have
placed itself as firmly on the map as Liverpool, London, Manchester
or Birmingham, it still boasted a few combos (with ever-changing
personnel) in the decade's first years. Lead guitarist Pete Watts fronted
The Sandstorms, who later became The Anchors, by which time they'd
acquired drummer Terry (Terence Dale) Griffin: sometimes known as 'The
little snigger buffin', or 'Buffin' for short. Further name and personnel
changes saw The Anchors become Wild Dog's Hell Hounds in 1963,
The Soulents in early-1964 and The Silence in 1965. Les Norman led
another local group – The Buddies – on vocals and rhythm guitar, with
Mick Ralphs on lead guitar and vocals, though when asked whether he
played rhythm or lead, he would modestly insist that he didn't know:
'I just play guitar'. Vocalist Stan Tippins replaced Les, and their bassist
Des Grubb moved on, with Cyril Townsend and then Pete Watts taking
up the vacancy. The Buddies then became The Problem, with the usual
ever-shifting lineup. The Problem was just one of several names they
would resort to when travelling to and from Germany and Italy, as
they sometimes had to leave under difficult circumstances that meant
returning under a different name would be advisable. In 1966 they
became The Doc Thomas Group with Stan, Mick and Pete – the latter now
playing bass – joined by Dave Tedstone on guitar, and Bob Hall on drums.

Like many other British groups working the pub and club circuit, their
repertoire was built largely on pop versions of soul hits such as 'I Got
You', 'She Was Really Saying Something', 'Rescue Me', 'I'll Be Doggone'
and 'Barefootin''. Gigs in mainland Europe – mainly in Hamburg and Italy
– led to a couple of residencies and, more importantly, a record contract
with the Italian Interrecord label. In October 1966, they entered a studio
in Milan and taped several cover songs taken from their setlist. Two of
the numbers – 'Just Can't Go To Sleep' (a Ray Davies song from the first
Kinks album) and 'Harlem Shuffle' – appeared on a single and, a year
or two later, an album including ten other tracks from the same session.
For a while, some of the group were also part of The Shakedown Sound,
backing Jimmy Cliff – a Jamaican singer brought over to England by Chris
Blackwell, who, as the head of Island Records, would shortly play an
important part in their career. Organist Terry Allen was part of this group,

and in 1968, The Shakedown Sound – now comprising Stan, Mick, Pete, Dale and Terry – became Silence.

They were now writing and playing more original material, influenced largely by progressive rock and West-Coast-influenced psychedelia. An agency based in Swansea had booked the group plenty of gigs in South Wales, and they were building up a good following. But the agency withdrew its support when the group said they no longer wanted to play only cover versions, so they moved to London to further their ambitions. Hungry for success, they recorded some demos and pitched them to EMI, Polydor and Immediate, but without any luck. Calling themselves The Archers, they next tried Apple Records, but like before, got no further.

In May 1969, Free, who had just released their first album, were thought to be on the point of splitting in two, with vocalist Paul Rodgers and bassist Andy Fraser planning to leave and form their own band, while guitarist Paul Kossoff and drummer Simon Kirke planned to replace them with new members. Guy Stevens – head of A & R at Island Records – placed an ad in *Melody Maker* asking for a bass player, and Pete went along, taking Mick with him for moral support. Pete ended up jamming with Kossoff and Kirke, and Guy was very impressed, although whether it was his bass skills or his long hair, knee boots and buckskin jacket that made the most impact, was open to debate. When Pete mentioned that his group Silence was looking for a contract, Guy also seemed interested in that. As subsequent events would soon show, the *split* in Free was either a swiftly-resolved difference of opinion or a matter of Guy finding two of the members too headstrong for his liking, and deciding it might be better to fire and replace them before they knew what was happening.

Whatever the truth of it, Pete was not required as Free's new bassist, but the contact he'd made with the maverick Mr. Stevens was shortly to prove fruitful. As a result, Mick contacted Guy, who felt that any band with somebody like Pete in their lineup *must* have potential, and arranged an audition. He took a Silence demo tape to Island Records, and sat in the offices for about three hours, becoming increasingly annoyed by the attitude of the condescending receptionists. Later, he walked into Guy's office and vented his wrath at being messed around. It struck the right note with Guy, whose response was 'Come in, I like your attitude.' Without bothering to hear the demos, he booked an audition for Silence in a third-floor office at Spot Studio in South Molton Street. When the audition time came, Guy was staggered to see them dragging a huge Hammond organ up the narrow stairs. If they were determined to go to such lengths to prove their worth, he said he did not care what they sounded like – he was going to sign them.

Though after that, the audition was a mere formality, the group played a few originals written separately by Mick and Pete, along with their versions of psychedelic numbers from the likes of Strawberry Alarm Clock and The Electric Flag. Guy thought they were great musicians but felt that Stan – as a non-instrument-playing singer – didn't seem too comfortable with the material. He'd been known in Italy as 'The Sinatra of beat', and his voice was more suited to mainstream pop in the mould of an English Tom Jones, rather than the more contemporary, progressive style the others were aiming for. When told that he was not an ideal fit, Stan took it in good part, magnanimously telling the rest of the group that he'd never stand in the way of them getting a deal.

Guy had this vision of a new group with the lyrical strengths of Bob Dylan, the rhythm section and general swagger of The Rolling Stones, and the keyboard stylings of Procol Harum. He had already played a considerable role in the success story of the latter, having introduced lyricist Keith Reid to keyboard player Gary Brooker, supplied them with their band name (that of a friend's pedigree cat) and inspired them to write their first major song after hearing a friend at a party say, 'You've just turned a whiter shade of pale'. When he tried to sign Procol Harum to Island, Chris Blackwell turned them down, so they went elsewhere with a classic debut single that went on to top the British charts for six weeks.

Fast-forward to summer 1969 when Guy placed an advertisement in *Melody Maker* – on behalf of Island Records who needed a pianist/singer 'to join exciting hard rock band playing Bob-Dylan-influenced country rock music' – and promising immediate album-recording work. One person who enquired about the position of vocalist was former Screaming Lord Sutch keyboard player Freddie 'Fingers' Lee, who turned it down, deciding the paltry wages being offered were an insult to his talents. He said he was earning more in Germany nightly than Island would pay him in a week.

A few hopefuls were auditioned at Regent Sound Studio but were found wanting for one reason or another. Despondently, the group took a break and went out to a local café. On returning, studio manager Bill Farley said he knew someone who might be interested.

When he made the call, on the other end of the phone was Ian Hunter Patterson. Born in Shrewsbury in 1939, he was several years older than the Silence members, although, in the best music business tradition, he became one of several who subtracted about five years from their age when music journalists asked what it was.

In his formative years, his horizons changed from the inevitability of a life of manual or factory labour, when he heard records by Jerry Lee Lewis and Little Richard – that was all the inspiration he needed to think again. His first steps towards a music career came while staying at a Butlin's holiday camp one summer when he befriended Colin York and Colin Broom: two fellow visitors of a similar age to him. Just for fun, they entered a talent competition, performing 'Blue Moon' accompanying themselves on acoustic guitars. Both Colins were members of The Apex: an amateur outfit based in Northampton. Sometimes known as The Group, they made a single in 1961 and an EP on the John Lever label three years later – John Lever being the drummer and owner of a local record shop. Ian joined The Apex from time to time on rhythm guitar, though he was not a member when the two records were made. Further stints followed, with Hurricane Henry and The Shriekers – another local band, fronted by Freddie Lee – and with The Savages, on guitar, and later, piano.

By this time, Ian was married with two children, taking a succession of jobs in order to make ends meet and provide for his family. These included employment in factories, digging roads, and as a journalist with a local newspaper. The new band played a few gigs in Hamburg clubs, similar to those in which The Beatles had served their apprenticeship at the start of the 1960s. Brief stints with various other groups followed, including a New Yardbirds put together by Mickie Most after the demise of the successful mid-1960s outfit of the same name. This led to a belief that Ian had been a member of Led Zeppelin in their early days, but in fact, there were also one or two other 'New Yardbirds' on the live circuit, this being the Jimmy Page-led one that changed their name and went on to find global fame and fortune.

Though he also played bass and piano, Ian decided that his gifts might be better suited to writing songs for music publishers, and he worked successively with Francis, Day & Hunter (a prescient name) and Leeds Music. His first recorded composition 'And I Have Learned To Dream' appeared on the B-side of a 1967 Dave Berry single. It was a dreamy psychedelic tune with distorted vocals, and though the A-side was a new song written by the up-and-coming Bee Gees, it failed to chart.

When not working in the publishers' offices trying to write that elusive future chart contender, he continued playing with At Last The 1958

Rock and Roll Show, again led by Freddie Lee. They released two singles in 1968 – 'I Can't Drive' on CBS, and after a name-change to Charlie Woolfe, 'Dance Dance Dance' on NEMS. The B-side of the latter – 'Home' – had a three-way writing credit of Lee (under his real name Frederick Cheesman), guitarist Miller Anderson and Ian Patterson. After Lee died in 2014, Ian paid tribute to him on his website, saying he would always be grateful to the man who had given him some hope for a musical career at a time when he thought the factory was his only future: 'I'll always remember him saying to me, "You're a good songwriter, but don't ever try to sing". He was probably right!'

A passionate lover of rock and roll music and the work of Bob Dylan, Ian had little confidence in his vocal ability but knew he could write songs as well as play guitar and other instruments. Nevertheless, he presented himself at the Island Records audition performing Sonny Bono's 'Laugh At Me' and Dylan's 'Like A Rolling Stone'.

The rest of the group felt that though Ian was not really a singer, was hardly a piano player and had little fashion sense, there was something different about him – the vocal meant more to him than just singing someone else's lyrics, and as Mick later recalled, 'he had the look'. Perversely, again according to Mick, it was partly the shades Ian wore to conceal what he self-deprecatingly called his 'fat face', that worked in his favour. Guy thought they helped give him the right image and told him he ought to keep them on in future.

After Ian left the audition, the rest of them had a chat and decided he was better than everyone else, but that he wasn't exactly what they had in mind. Guy said they should get him in for a couple of weeks so they could tell Island they had a complete group, then find someone better and give him the sack. However, they had evidently given up the search, and Ian was in. Ironically, at first, he found that they all seemed very insular – a local band from Hereford in a big city – and the only one who would talk to him at first was Stan. Having been not-unwillingly fired – or rather, asked to step aside – Stan stayed on as a faithful tour manager, trusted friend and occasional backing vocalist, remaining a part of their entourage for many years. Ian – the last to join – would now be the frontman, the face and voice of the group.

Chapter One: 1969-1970

On 5 June 1969, the group signed a contract, significantly with Guy Stevens, not Island Records – Fred Griffin adding his signature on behalf of his son Dale who was not quite 21. Rehearsals were due to begin four days later at the Pied Bull in Islington. With Mick and Pete, there were already two writers in the band, and though Ian's work for a music publisher had required him to come up with more middle-of-the-road fare, he eagerly took up the challenge of writing for a different market altogether. Guy told him that they wanted Bob Dylan type lyrics, Dylan being one of those writers who could not really sing – rather like Leonard Cohen and Randy Newman – yet who had a compelling delivery. Ian readily obliged, coming up with numbers like 'Half Moon Bay' – a lengthy epic they worked on in their first rehearsal – 'Backsliding Fearlessly' and 'Road To Birmingham' – a song that attacked racism: Birmingham, in this case, referring to that in Alabama. When asked what had inspired the song, Ian said he thought it scandalous that the government should set up offices in Commonwealth countries to attract people to come and live in Britain and then treat them so badly when they arrived.

In addition to original material, at their first rehearsals, the band played Doug Sahm's 'At The Crossroads', Dylan's 'Can You Please Crawl Out Your Window' and Chuck Berry's 'Little Queenie', and Sonny Bono's 'Laugh At Me'. Yet it was soon evident they wouldn't need to rely so much on outside material. Miller Anderson – a singer and guitarist who played in bands with Ian in the early days and remained a friend – opined that Ian wrote such good songs because he'd packed so much into his 30 years outside of music. As Ian put it, anyone who left school and went straight into a band had no real-life experiences to write about, whereas *he* had about 40 jobs and eight years in factories before joining the group that would make him a household name.

Though on their first meeting, Ian may have given the others the impression of lacking that *je ne sais quoi*, he was not short on work ethic. He was nearly five years older than the next eldest member (Mick), almost four years Guy's senior and he already had a family. Daily rehearsal sessions went from 10:00 to 6:00, and Ian was punctual, seating himself at the piano to write new songs. Having had so many dead-end jobs, he knew this was his last shot. The others would roll in about four hours later, usually nursing hangovers, and somewhat less bothered, much to his annoyance. It was almost like a prefect trying to keep an unruly class in order.

The band needed a new name. 'Silence' was deemed not quite right, and for a while, they (or rather Guy) liked the idea of Savage Rose, Griff Fender, Brain Haulage and Blue Egg. When they began recording the first album, they were still Savage Rose & Fixable, until Guy found that Savage Rose (after a character in the sleeve notes for Dylan's *Highway 61 Revisited*) had been appropriated by a Danish group. Further inspiration was not long in coming. While serving a prison sentence on drugs charges a little earlier, Guy had read a novel by Willard Manus – *Mott The Hoople* – about a character who lived two miles from heaven. They needed to look no further, and on 27 June the band name became Mott the Hoople.

Guy intended for his proteges to hit the ground running. Whereas most other groups would've been sent on tour for several weeks so they could get to know the material and hammer their sound into shape in a baptism of fire, Mott were booked into North London's Morgan Recording Studios on 20 June, after eleven days of rehearsal and not one gig behind them. Guy had decided he would produce their first album. He said there were only two Phil Spectors, and he was one of them. Ian later reminisced that Guy was indeed like Spector, but without the musical knowledge. Guy had always had a passion for music, having built up one of the finest collections of obscure imported R&B and blues records in England. The fact that he could neither sing in tune nor play an instrument to save his life, hardly seemed to matter. Full of ideas and vision, he could pull things out of the people he believed in, Ian being one of them. One thing Guy did *not* lack was encouragement, as he constantly urged the group on. Dale later said that his attitude to them was 'You are the Rolling Stones! You are Bob Dylan! You are up there with them! You are better than them!'. If he really and passionately believed in the band, there was no reason why they shouldn't believe in themselves. He got them drunk, they would play a load of rubbish, and he would tell them in all seriousness that it was 'great'.

Most of the recording was complete by the end of July. Mooted titles for the album were *Talking Bear Mountain Picnic Massacre Disaster Blues* (a minor variation on an early Dylan song, 'Talkin' Bear Mountain Picnic Massacre Blues') and *The Twilight of Pain Through Doubt*. In the end, they settled on using the group name.

Mott The Hoople (1969)

Personnel:

Ian Hunter: lead vocals, piano

Mick Ralphs: vocals, lead guitar
Overend Watts: bass, backing vocals
Verden Allen: organ, backing vocals
Dale Griffin: drums, backing vocals
Producer: Guy Stevens
Engineer: Andy Johns
Studio: Morgan Studios, Willesden, June-September 1969
Release date: November 1969
Chart placings: UK: 62, US: 185
Running time: 37:08
Side One: 1. You Really Got Me (Ray Davies) 2. At The Crossroads (Doug Sahm)
3. Laugh At Me (Sonny Bono) 4. Backsliding Fearlessly (Hunter)
Side Two: 1. Rock And Roll Queen (Ralphs) 2. Rabbit Foot And Toby Time (Ralphs)
3. Half Moon Bay (Hunter / Ralphs) 4. Wrath and Wroll (Stevens)
Bonus tracks: Angel Air (2003)
9. Ohio (Live) (Neil Young) 10. Find Your Way (Ralphs)

Delivering a debut album that began with three cover versions was
perhaps an indication of how the group were still finding their feet and
were unsure of their songwriting abilities. The first was an explosive
instrumental version of 'You Really Got Me', a song they were inspired
to try after watching The Kinks arriving for work one day at Pye Studios.
Building on the basic guitar riff, they turned it into a powerhouse hard-
rock juggernaut, initially with vocals (by Mick) and then without. It was
followed by Doug Sahm's 'At the Crossroads': a bittersweet country ballad
of love, loss and aching regret. Ian's yearning vocal finds the perfect
setting in the subdued rhythm and slide guitar, later supplemented by an
evocative soundscape of organ and piano culminating in a rich crescendo,
calling to mind *Blonde On Blonde*-era Dylan, and Procol Harum. The
track brought Mott a wider audience through its inclusion on Island
Records' various-artists budget-price sampler *Nice Enough To Eat*, and the
track was said to have been much-admired by Dylan himself.

The third in this cover trilogy was 'Laugh At Me', which progressed
from a peaceful piano intro to an all-guns-blazing power ballad, with
an instrumental coda for the last two of its six-plus minutes. With its
remarkable marriage of guitar, piano and organ, it compared favourably
with Dylan's 'Like A Rolling Stone' and another rock epic coincidentally
released that same month: The Rolling Stones' 'You Can't Always Get
What You Want' (B-side of 'Honky Tonk Women').

Side one ended with the first original number. Ian's 'Backsliding Fearlessly' – a title supplied by Guy (original title, 'If the World Saluted You') – was packed with doom-laden images – 'Three cheers for the innocent though he is perverse/Three screams for the hangman as he cries for the hearse'. It was a folky waltz that clearly bore the inspiration of Dylan's 'The Times They Are A-Changin''.

With the album almost complete, Guy realised it lacked an out-and-out rock number. A quick call to Mick and Ian resulted in the former's 'Rock And Roll Queen' – written and recorded in September with Ian on vocal – opening side two. In Mick's words, it was 'a fictitious story written about being on the road in America, using a load of clichés'. He also contributed 'Rabbit Foot And Toby Time': a two-minute instrumental with guitar and organ predominating.

'Half Moon Bay' is the record's most spectacular moment, albeit a lengthy one. At eleven epic minutes, it's the longest track they would ever release. Ian commented that he was playing songs backwards and reversed chords on piano, with Guy egging him on, and the result was one of the best things he had ever done: 'All the jumbled ingredients of those early days, thrown together in one bizarre track'. The lyrics are 'just visual words' with no reference to the title. Musically, much of it is set to a rolling three-chord pattern driven by subdued piano, the swirling organ sea effect (more Procol Harum similarities), and halfway through, a break with variations on Beethoven's 'Piano Sonata No. 14' ('Moonlight Sonata'). Towards the climax come a few sound effects or possibly chords, imitating a helicopter.

The album finishes with the 90-second jam 'Wrath and Roll'. Doubtless, with an eye on royalties, Guy claimed the writing credit for this, as he edited it from a tape of a fifteen-minute jam of 'You Really Got Me'. Several different versions of the latter were recorded, with some released many years later, including an eleven-minute instrumental and a three-minute vocal take.

Guy was not only responsible for some of the song titles, but for renaming at least three band members on the sleeve. Ian Hunter Patterson dropped the family name and became Ian Hunter, organist Terence Allen became Verden Allen (his father's name had been Verdun), and bassist Pete Watts used his middle name, Overend. Mick somehow escaped intact, but drummer Dale Griffin's nickname Buffin was used on their album sleeves for the next few years.

The sleeve design – again Guy's idea – was based on a drawing of lizards by Dutch graphic artist M. C. Escher. On the back was a motif of a reptile eating its own tail: something rock critics would later consider prescient in light of the group's subsequent history. One idea they originally had was to include a picture of Bob Dylan on the sleeve before deciding this might be taking the fixation with their hero a little too far. Another of Guy's rather over-ambitious plans was to make the album a double, with 'You Really Got Me' stretching out to eleven minutes. Other tracks recorded but shelved included Mick's 'Little Christine' (which Dale later described as 'a cautionary tale of love and shifty shenanigans in the Old West') and Chuck Berry's 'Little Queenie'. In America, Chicago (formerly Chicago Transit Authority, until the company of the same name threatened court action) broke all the rules by making their first three albums doubles (from 1969 to 1971), on the condition that they accepted a lower royalty rate. But for a not-yet tried-and-tested British group to begin their recording career thus, would've likely never secured label agreement.

Although the *Mott The Hoople* album was, to a large extent, experimental and anything *but* commercial, some regard it as the best of the group's Island releases. Verden said that for him, it was the finest of their albums, recorded on eight-track with no messing about. They went into the studio, laid the basic tracks down, 'and maybe something went on afterwards, like the vocal', but much of it was a spontaneous collective effort. Overend also recalled the sessions being straightforward, and most of the songs were recorded in one take.

'Rock And Roll Queen' b/w 'Road To Birmingham' was released as a single in October 1969 to negligible airplay and, subsequently, poor sales. The first 5,000 copies inadvertently included 'Road To Birmingham' as side one's last track, with 'Backsliding Fearlessly' replacing 'Rock And Roll Queen' on side two – before the error was noticed and amended for subsequent pressings.

The group signed with Atlantic Records for American distribution and the album was released there in spring 1970. In Britain, critical reaction was generally favourable, invoking complimentary comparisons with Dylan and Led Zeppelin, although Mott had to wait five months before the album enjoyed one solitary week in the album chart.

Next, Mott The Hoople got down to some serious gigging. In retrospect, Ian admitted it was probably fortuitous that the album preceded live performance. He thought their early shows were pretty bad, and Island might've dropped them had the album – the recording costs of which went well over budget – not already been in the can. On 2 August 1969, they went to Italy for a seven-day residency at the Bat Caverna Club, Riccione, to begin on 6 August. The first night, they went down really well, as Ian was fumbling and playing 'bad chords', and the audience thought he was blind. When word got out after the show that he could actually see perfectly well, they lost interest and gave the band a less sympathetic reception. Within four days, the promoter told them they were on half pay, or they could go home. They reluctantly accepted the fee cut and treated the remaining shows like a rehearsal.

Back in England, they played their first home gig at Romford Market Hall, London, on 5 September, supporting Island labelmates King Crimson. Guy had devised a stage act whereby Mick and Overend would do the onstage patter while Ian sat quietly at his piano 'like an albino Ray Charles'. After each number, tables of DJs near the front (who Guy had invited) clapped reverently while the rest of the audience watched in disbelief. A second gig – supporting Free (another Island act) at Sunderland – went a little better. Over the next few weeks, they gradually gained confidence, especially when they realised that the faster songs went down better than the slower ones. But still being short of material, they played some songs twice in a set, and 'You Really Got Me' sometimes became a marathon 20-minute jam.

An early and influential convert to the Mott cause was journalist Pete Frame, who that April had started writing, editing and publishing *ZigZag* – the first important British monthly rock magazine, following in the tradition of America's *Rolling Stone*. Guy sent him a test pressing of the *Mott The Hoople* album, and Frame was completely blown away. When he was invited to meet the group at the Island offices, they all got on very well, and his admiration only increased after he saw them live for the first time in November at the Country Club, Hampstead. Frame said the group inspired passion, their songs were based on reality, and Ian Hunter was 'almost Byronic' in his poet's view of the world – being totally unlike 'those whimsical singer-songwriter folk poets', he had instead experienced so much and had far wider horizons.

As Mott's reputation spread by word-of-mouth and their exposure increased through live performance, they landed their first radio and television appearances. In February 1970, they recorded the first of two BBC Radio 1 sessions, consisting of 'Laugh At Me', 'At the Crossroads' and 'Thunderbuck Ram'. It served as an audition for a BBC panel, which unanimously passed what they called in their notes 'this Dylan-influenced group', and it was broadcast on John Peel's *Top Gear* later that month.

The session went smoothly, except for their irritation with producer John Walters, who sat at the controls reading his newspaper while they were running through their songs. When they asked him which songs he wanted them to do, he replied 'the shortest ones' without enthusiasm. That same month, they played 'At the Crossroads' on BBC TV's *Disco 2*: a precursor of *The Old Grey Whistle Test*. The group felt they were making progress, although, in retrospect, Ian later said that they were going against the grain, 'because it was all blues and then the hippie thing happened', and they fitted comfortably in neither category.

Further radio exposure came in April and October when they recorded concerts for Radio 1 at London's Paris Theatre. Mick found the atmosphere a little inhibiting, likening it to being back at school, saying they were made to feel they should not be too loud or wild, 'because it wasn't acceptable'. It *was,* however, preferable to a live television show they played in Paris around the same time. One audience member threw something at Ian, whereupon Overend kicked the guy in the head – 'It got nasty' and the incident made the papers the next day, with the French press labelling them 'animals'.

In between gigs, the group recorded their second album, which had the original working title of *Sticky Fingers*. Comprising five songs by Ian and two by Mick, it was a more difficult album to make than the first. According to Ian, around the time of release, they were in a peculiar mood, 'and we went into the studio with the numbers but no lyrics written – they just came as we recorded'. Later he said he was embarrassed by it, as it was badly produced, badly mixed, and 'We were all mental when we did it'. Guy – who was on speed when he mixed it – bore some of the responsibility. Unlike the first album, *Mad Shadows* was the end result of eight or nine studio sessions spread over about six months.

Mad Shadows (1970)

Personnel:
Ian Hunter: lead vocals, piano, rhythm guitar
Mick Ralphs: vocals, lead guitar
Overend Watts: bass, backing vocals
Verden Allen: organ, backing vocals
Dale Griffin: drums, backing vocals
Guy Stevens: spiritual percussion, psychic piano

Producer: Guy Stevens
Engineer: Andy Johns
Studio: Olympic Studios, London, November 1969-April 1970
Release date: 25 September 1970
Chart placing: UK: 48
Running time: 35:51
Side One: 1. Thunderbuck Ram (Ralphs) 2. No Wheels To Ride (Hunter) 3. You Are
One Of Us (Hunter) 4. Walkin' With A Mountain (Hunter)
Side Two: 1. I Can Feel (Hunter) 2. Threads Of Iron (Ralphs) 3. When My Mind's
Gone (Hunter)
Bonus tracks, Angel Air (2003)
8. It Would Be a Pleasure (Ralphs) 9. How Long? (Death May Be Your Santa Claus)
(Hunter / Allen)

There are only two out-and-out rock and roll numbers on *Mad Shadows*.
The first – 'Thunderbuck Ram' – is topped and tailed by powerful guitar
riffing (cue comparisons with Fleetwood Mac's 'Oh Well') and Mick's
intense vocal. The piano is fairly prominent, but Verden's organ was
pushed down in the final mix until almost inaudible, except in the last
30 seconds or so. He was so frustrated that when they all listened to the
completed album at Guy's Swiss Cottage flat, Verden destroyed a test
pressing in front of everyone – an outburst that was enough for Guy to
attempt to fire him until it was met with fierce resistance from the others,
who threatened to sack *Guy* and find another producer next time.

From there on, the album is rather top-heavy, Ian's slower, introspective
songs largely dominating. 'No Wheels To Ride' is the anguished lament
of a weary traveller – its six minutes full of light and shade, piano and
haunting organ backing subdued verses, building to a frenzied chorus,
and punctuated by incendiary guitar breaks halfway through and at the
end. 'You Are One Of Us' – edited from five minutes to half the length –
is a moody reflection on the group's relationship with their fans and a
thank-you to them.

Closing side one is the Chuck-Berry-flavoured 'Walkin' With a Mountain'
– Ian's sole rocker on the album – written quickly during a tea break.
Thought to have been inspired by the old Spike Milligan track 'I'm
Walking Out With a Mountain', it's the sound of a band cutting free and
really enjoying themselves. Mick Jagger dropped into the studio and
danced around while they were playing it, so after the last chorus, Ian
broke spontaneously into 'Jumpin' Jack Flash', before they jammed

towards the fadeout. The song would become a favourite at gigs and remain in Ian's live repertoire for many years.

Side two is a sombre, even quite chilling affair. The seven-minute gospel-tinged 'I Can Feel' is a doomy reflection on living on borrowed time in a hostile world, with a quiet Procol Harum organ-driven verse one moment and an intense chorus the next – and for those with sharp ears and a good pair of headphones, a squeaking drum foot pedal and a missed beat due to a broken stick. They wanted to re-record it, but Guy insisted it was perfect as it stood.

'Threads of Iron' starts as a mid-tempo poppy number with Ian and Mick sharing vocals, then morphing into a one-chord jam with a splendid disorderly finish. Finally, 'When My Mind's Gone' is a six-minute stream of consciousness that Ian made up with two piano chords in his head, and sang as they went along, with the minimal accompaniment of organ and bass. Guy encouraged him to keep going and just sing and play anything, hence the sleeve credit for 'Spiritual percussion and psychic piano'. After completing it in one take, there was silence... then Guy pushed the switch down in the control room and started screaming.

Mad Shadows is a strange, unsettling, intense yet fascinating, and honest album. A stark black and white sleeve design enhances the mood, with a kaleidoscopic mirror-image of a smoking fire grate (resembling a hideously distorted, demonic face) on the front. The inner-gatefold shows *Peace* – Victorian artist William Strutt's 1896 lithograph of an innocent-looking child surrounded by farm animals and a friendly lion: a prophecy of the second coming from the Book of Isaiah. On the back is Ian's double mirror-image profile. There's no picture of the other band members anywhere – Guy's photo-shoot idea involving all five members dressed in druid's cloaks with silver foil obscuring their heads having been aborted. Above the two-headed Ian are a few apocalyptic lines from a Baudelaire poem: the source of the album title.

Written and recorded more or less live in the studio, *Mad Shadows* is in some parts the equivalent of John Lennon's primal scream album: coincidentally, recorded about the time this was released. Ian later said that the record was him 'egoing out' – the others were trying to play, and he was 'all over it', out of control, his voice little more than a croak at times. Above all, it was badly produced and mixed. He felt bad for them, as 'They went along with it, but their hearts weren't in it'. Though chaotic and shambolic, *Mad Shadows* is – despite the negatives – a strange, unvarnished record that somehow holds together.

Mott were keen to release a single from the album – to follow in the vein of labelmates Free, who were riding high with the number two single 'All Right Now' and the number two album *Fire And Water* – and broaden their appeal, but it never happened.

Mad Shadows was originally the working title for a solo album by Island artist Steve Winwood, but his project gradually morphed into an album by the newly-reconvened Traffic – *John Barleycorn Must Die* – so *Mad Shadows* was up for grabs. It was fortuitous, as Guy had long been friendly with The Rolling Stones. When he told them about Mott's original working title *Sticky Fingers*, they liked it so much that they used it for their next album.

As *Mad Shadows* was being prepared for release, Mott The Hoople undertook a nine-week American tour from May to July, supporting the likes of Ten Years After, Traffic, The Kinks, Jethro Tull, Mountain, Freddie King and Albert King. Mott's debut album had just been issued stateside; FM stations were playing it regularly, and the American audiences were really receptive. Dale recalled that both Kings were 'fine players and real gentlemen'. Albert introduced the band on stage every night, but never quite got the hang of their name – they might be Martha's Hoppers, Matt The Hoof Off or Mother's Hoobles.

One tour incident that could've descended into serious unpleasantness came when Guy – who, as their manager, insisted on accompanying the band on tour, despite their reservations – sat in with them on a radio interview that also included The Kinks. Guy found the latter very close-knit and insular, didn't have much respect for them in the first place, and, to Mott's embarrassment, went out of his way to goad them. When one of The Kinks said he preferred playing football to being in a rock group, Guy swore at him and told him he didn't deserve to be in a group. All of Mott were amazed that The Kinks took it quite placidly instead of getting up and thumping him.

At the time, Mott concluded their live act with a raving version of 'You Really Got Me' that lasted up to 20 minutes or so. On the dates when they supported The Kinks, Ian recalled they had to warn Ray Davies that if he didn't let them play the song, they could only do half an hour before The Kinks came on. Davies was fine about letting them do it but couldn't resist poking a little gentle fun at them in front of the audience. When The Kinks played a medley at the end of their set, Ray said with a smile that this would give 'The Hoople' a chance to figure out which song they could nick next time.

On Mott's previous America tour, Atlantic Records provided helpful support and promotion, but the band felt that interest in them was diminishing after they played a showcase gig in June supporting Traffic at Stony Brook University on Long Island, New York. Ahmet Ertegun – the head of Atlantic – and Chris Blackwell came to the gig together. Everything was fine until the band started playing without a soundcheck: the regular bugbear of any non-headlining act. Only then did they realise that Verden's Hammond organ was horribly out of tune with Ian's electric piano – partly a result of the difference in the number of cycles American electricity ran at compared with the UK standard. There was no chance of them using Traffic's Hammond, so they carried on the best they could. Needless to say, with his sharp musical ear, Ertegun was all too aware of the difficulty. They all thought he should've known they were the victims of a technical problem and possibly some chicanery calculated to make them come across badly. With that, they decided resignedly that their chances in America would be slender.

Because of his drink and drug issues, the group never found Guy easy to work with, let alone have him as their manager. Ian once said that Guy was meant to be 'managing' them, but *they* had to be the ones to help *him* get out of bed. At various times Guy would try to get rid of one or other of them. More than once, he told them that Ian had to leave, and they should get Graham Bell – vocalist with Heavy Jelly – to replace him. Overend said Ian rivalled Guy as a creative force, was writing more and more good songs and 'was trying to take over the group', also possibly being rude to Guy on occasion. The others always defended Ian on the grounds that he was merely doing what Guy asked him to by writing Dylan-and-Stones-type songs. Ian had willingly and uncomplainingly taken on the responsibility of coming up with a plentiful supply of original material, and the others were happy to let him carry on.

Conversely, the group *were* growing in confidence, and the live shows were improving all the time. Mick reckoned they were 'a pre-punk punk band who just went on and went berserk'; very rough around the edges, but they never failed to make contact with the audience, and always put on an exciting show. They claimed to be trendsetters in that they went for dynamic clothing that showed up well on stage. This was not lost on the likes of Marc Bolan, Slade and Elton John, who would all become sartorial trendsetters in the approaching glam rock era. Status Quo were also Mott fans and came to see their shows. According to Verden, that was how the Quo got the idea of shaking their heads up and down – a stage idea that helped them change their image from a pop group to a heavyweight rock band.

1970 was the year of live albums by The Who and The Rolling Stones. With the same objective in mind, Mott decided to record two shows supporting Free on 13 September at Croydon's Fairfield Halls. They used a portable eight-track machine borrowed from The Who, but the audience besieged the stage, wrecked the cables, and for many years it was thought that very little material could be salvaged.

Mad Shadows grazed the album charts for two weeks that autumn, but the group realised something had to change if they were going to make the major league. In October, they made another TV appearance on *Disco 2*, playing 'Walkin' With A Mountain' and 'Rock And Roll Queen'. A second BBC *In Concert* for Radio 1 followed, with the group adding to their set Ian's new song 'The Debt', and Neil Young's angry 'Ohio': written in response to the Kent State shootings in which four college students were killed earlier that year.

Meanwhile, after the debacle resulting from the mixing of *Mad Shadows*, they decided to produce their third album themselves. In musical terms, Mick would be in the driving seat. The songs would be less intense and look more towards a West Coast country-rock style. As Ian once remarked, if he was Dylan and The Stones, Mick was Stephen Stills. The album's working title was *Original Mixed-Up Mott*, but in the end, they settled for *Wildlife*, recorded mostly over the last two months of 1970.

Chapter Two: 1971

With only the briefest break over Christmas and new-year, 1971 began with no let-up in the live schedule. Towards the end of January, Mott The Hoople played their first dates as a headlining act, supported by Wishbone Ash. The latter were promoting their eponymous debut album, which simultaneously reached the Top 30. The groups bonded well, and Overend got on particularly well with Ash bass player Martin Turner, not least as the latter bought one of Overend's guitars. The calendar remained full, with shows in Britain up until April, except for five Sweden shows in February. It was a period that would see the release of their third album.

Wildlife *(1971)*
Personnel:
Ian Hunter: lead vocals, piano, rhythm guitar
Mick Ralphs: vocals, lead guitar
Overend Watts: bass, backing vocals
Verden Allen: organ, backing vocals
Dale Griffin: drums, backing vocals
Additional personnel:
Jerry Hogan: steel guitar
Jess Roden, Stan Tippins: backing vocals
London Symphony Orchestra: arranged and conducted by Michael Gray
Jim Archer: violin
Producers: Mott The Hoople/Guy Stevens
Engineer: Brian Humphries
Studio: Island Studios, Basing Street, London, September-December 1970
Release date: March 1971
Chart placing: UK: 44
Running time: 38:25
Side One: 1. Whisky Women (Ralphs) 2. Angel Of Eighth Avenue (Hunter) 3. Wrong Side Of The River (Ralphs) 4. Waterlow (Hunter) 5. Lay Down (Melanie Safka).
Side Two: 1. It Must Be Love (Ralphs) 2. Original Mixed-Up Kid (Hunter) 3. Home Is Where I Want to Be (Ralphs) 4. Keep A-Knockin' (Richard Penniman)
Bonus tracks: Angel Air (2003)
10. It'll Be Me (Jack Clement) 11. Long Red (Leslie West / Felix Pappalardi / John Ventura / Norman Landsberg)

Three tracks from September 1970 – Mick's 'Wrong Side Of The River' (a leftover from the *Mad Shadows* sessions), a cover of Melanie Safka's 'Lay Down', and 'Keep A-Knockin'' from the Croydon gig – supplemented three more songs from Mick and another three from Ian: one co-written with Verden. Mick's 'Whisky Women' – originally called 'Brain Haulage' – opened the album. It was inspired by the Los Angeles club Whisky a Go Go – a magnet for rock stars and groupies alike. This song and 'Wrong Side Of The River' – a slower, reflective song with shimmering organ alongside piano and acoustic guitar – showed a marked Crosby, Stills, Nash & Young influence: Neil Young's vocal style, particularly in the second song. 'It Must be Love', a brisk, bustling country-rock song – with Jerry Hogan's steel guitar adding colour – clearly has the stamp of Buffalo Springfield and Poco. The last of Mick's songs on the album – 'Home Is Where I Want to Be' – is an unashamedly soul-baring country-folk number about missing the security of home while on the road, and longing to be back in Hereford.

Ian's three songs follow a similar introspective line. 'Angel Of Eighth Avenue' was about meeting a girl from the Bronx who had escaped from a difficult family life and an abusive relationship. Ian wrote it after a drunken evening in Greenwich Village while on tour the previous year. It's a bittersweet, largely acoustic guitar and organ ballad, complemented with violin. The song reflected how Ian felt that morning as he looked out his Manhattan hotel window at the street below him, thinking how it was his first trip to America and he could hardly believe he was there: 'and then she came and stood beside me'.

Originally called 'Blue Broken Tears', 'Waterlow' – named after a North London park where Ian used to take his children – is a heartrending tale of love and loss that came out of the separation and subsequent divorce from his first wife. The London Symphony Orchestra's delicate and strong arrangement enhances the poignant mood.

Finally, 'Original Mixed-Up Kid' is an autobiographical lyric about Ian's confused rites of passage while growing up: 'In a crowded street, he can just see the sleet/While others see the snow'. It also has something of Mick's West-Coast vibe, with Jerry Hogan's steel guitar giving a decidedly Byrds-like flavour.

Of the two non-originals, 'Lay Down' was a gospel-flavoured song that writer Melanie Safka recorded with The Edwin Hawkins Singers. Mott followed the original faithfully and considered their version for a single release. The album closes with 'Keep A-Knockin'': a blistering – if shambolic – live cut from the Croydon gig. It interpolates fragments of Ray Charles' 'I Got A Woman', 'What I'd Say' and Jerry Lee Lewis's 'Whole Lotta Shakin' Goin' On', while Ian tells the audience that rock and roll is the best possible form of music that ever was. After about nine minutes – as what's turned into an unwieldy jam spirals out of control – it grinds to a halt, as he admits, 'This is a disaster area up here. I don't know what we're doing. Alright, well, we'll finish it now then'. One more chord brings it to a messy end.

The group initially admitted they were pleased with the album but later had second thoughts, referring to it less than affectionately as *'Mildlife'*. Dale said it was the most inept album they ever recorded, 'in terms of the engineer getting it wrong and insisting that we did it that way'. It was an interesting change of direction, if far less representative of their usual style. Remarking that 'Keep A-Knockin'' 'didn't quite fit', Ian said that the band always went down a storm live, but whenever they entered the studio, they always wanted to do quiet little songs instead. 'It didn't make any sense'. Ian also took to heart remarks the press made that the group couldn't really play their instruments because *Mad Shadows* seemed so rough and undisciplined – so on the subsequent album, it was as if they tried to go completely the other way. While he was knocked out with the songs on *Wildlife*, he said that overall it was too safe and very sterile. Having gone on record voicing his criticism of *Mad Shadows*, he later recanted, saying it was an honest record: 'a scream for help, but everyone was too embarrassed to say it'.

In *Rolling Stone*, Ben Edmonds gave the album an unequivocal thumbs-up. His review praised Mott for feeling sure enough of themselves to move away from the piano/organ-dominated sound of the first two albums and into country rock territory. He remarked that Ian's 'emory-board voice' had a habit of faltering under the strain of up-tempo songs, and was better suited to slower songs like 'Angel Of Eighth Avenue'. The spirited version of 'Lay Down' was an effective surprise, and 'Keep A-Knockin'', he opined, reminded him of the early Who.

A few additional tracks remained unreleased for some years, especially one that would eventually find a new life of its own, taped by Mick as a one-man-band. He arrived at the studio one day to find there was some confusion over the booking, and none of the others were going to be there. All the instruments had been mic'ed up and the tape was ready to roll. Rather than go home again, he spent several hours on a one-man demo playing guitars, drums, percussion, lead and backing vocals for a song he'd just written called 'Can't Get Enough Of Your Love'. It was destined to be a smash single, but not for Mott The Hoople.

Upon the third album's release, once again, their only reward would be a modest chart showing. In a music scene where the likes of Free, Deep Purple and Black Sabbath could have hit singles without turning themselves into teen stars, and where an American DJ could flip a new Rod Stewart 45 over to the B-side with 'Maggie May' and launch him into the stratosphere, Mott The Hoople were becoming increasingly desperate to elevate themselves into the big time on a similar trajectory, or at least achieve what they called 'quality singles success' like The Stones and The Who. The possibility of a more commercial re-recording of 'Lay Down' was discussed, but in the end, they decided that a new song written by Ian and Mick would be the answer.

Ian was inspired to come up with 'Midnight Lady' in New York while sitting on the lavatory, and a few ideas from Mick completed what they hoped would be their first hit. Initially called 'The Hooker' (not a title likely to find favour on the Radio 1 playlist or with TV programmers), and later 'Road To Rome', it had a memorable vocal hook and an infectious tune over two chords, which Verden's unmistakable organ work lifted in the first break with additional chords that pushed the melody frontier further out.

While touring America in spring 1971 – after a few gigs in Milwaukee on the same bill as Emerson, Lake & Palmer, and a round of Hell's Angels bars the night before that left Mott nursing hangovers – they flew to New York at the crack of dawn on 12 May for a session at Ultrasonic Studios. George 'Shadow' Morton – well-known for his work with such acts as The Shangri-Las and Vanilla Fudge – helmed the session. Like Guy Stevens, George had also battled a severe drink problem, and his best days were long since behind him. Steve Marriott was working in an adjoining studio that day and joined them – with the ever-dependable Stan Tippins – on backing vocals. The Humble Pie man's performance was so loud that he had to be isolated at the opposite end of the room. Among those present in a non-performing capacity was Ian's new American-Austrian girlfriend Trudi, who would later become his second wife.

Mott The Hoople were never averse to a little pleasant liquid-fuelled conviviality. But like true professionals, they accepted the importance of rarely, if ever, letting it make them any worse-for-wear on stage. They were resolutely anti-drugs, perhaps as a result of having seen their effect on Guy. Ian was particularly scathing of the endemic narcotics scene in America, particularly after he sat next to a young girl who started talking to him, reeled off a list of substances and seemed astonished when Ian denied ever having taken any of them.

It was to be a packed year for Mott The Hoople. In England, they'd been busy recording for the BBC, taping sessions in March for Mike Harding's *Sounds of the Seventies*, playing a couple of numbers on *Disco 2* in April, and on 6 July, recording a three-song session for John Peel's *Top Gear*. By this time, Free – the group who of late had been Island's hottest name – had split, though they soon reformed for what turned into a painful farewell.

Mott were attracting no end of positive music press coverage, in an era when there was still something a little uncool about being recognised as a hit-singles act (much as they yearned for that elusive top-tenner), and by consensus seemed to be one of England's most respected live acts. It was a reputation surely enhanced by their appearance two days after the Peel session, playing London's Royal Albert Hall. One reviewer compared the scene to that at the height of Beatlemania, with reports of several seats and boxes being broken by fans. The group were presented with an account for damages amounting to £1,467, and the venue management announced that, in view of the carnage, rock concerts would not be staged there in future. Ian long remembered it as his favourite Mott moment. He said the mainstream press and everyone else – or rather, 'the establishment' – hated them, but they had a devoted following who stuck with them through thick and thin. That night was the climax of all of them making a stand against the rest of the world, 'like a declaration of independence'.

Chris Charlesworth – who had long championed the band in the music press – in his review of the show for *Melody Maker*, suggested that Mott The Hoople were Britain's answer to Grand Funk but could play far better than the American three-piece. He called Ian 'the classic anti-hero' – the man who told the cheering audience that Led Zeppelin and Black Sabbath were on page one of the music papers. Mott themselves were on page nineteen, 'but that's where we belong'. For the encore, they had everyone going wild with 'Keep A-Knockin'', as usual. 'Musically, it's pretty disastrous, but no one cares'.

Mott were also banned from playing at Cheltenham Town Hall and Brighton Dome. In order to circumvent the possibility of future cancellations, they announced that they had acquired a 2,000-capacity mobile fibreglass theatre to perform in – the Caraivari – that could be erected on village greens around the country. The story made for good publicity, even though as a news item, it would've been more appropriate for release on April Fool's Day. There was clearly a tangible buzz about the group – as if massive success of top-10 single and album proportions was just round the corner.

On 9 July, 'Midnight Lady' b/w 'The Debt' was released as a single; the B-side was one of several numbers self-produced at Island Studios in April. A gentle Dylanesque Ian-written song with mainly acoustic guitar, organ and harmonica, Overend summed it up as 'puny and miserable'. But 'Midnight Lady' had a strong hook, and the music press were more than ready for it. In *NME*, Roy Carr wrote that it could do for Mott what 'All Right Now' did for Free – and with the sudden demise of the latter, he was sure that 'MTH will add Free's wandering following to their already swelling hordes'.

'Midnight Lady' also received the dubious accolade of being panned on Radio 1: by breakfast show presenter Tony Blackburn. Ian told audiences that if the DJ carried out his stated intention of hanging himself if the song was a hit, he wanted to be there as a witness.

On 22 July, Mott The Hoople filled the coveted new-release spot on BBC TV's *Top of the Pops*, and contrary to usual practice, the next day, it stopped selling. When it failed to chart, they admitted they were heartbroken but even more determined to make a second bid for what would surely be that game-changer.

Next time, they chose their version of Crazy Horse's 'Downtown' – a more poppy offering with Mick on vocals, recorded in the April sessions. Guy had come into the office one morning with a copy of the Crazy Horse album, saying the song would be just right for them. Upon its 17-September release, *NME* praised it, noting that it was 'handled with great relish by the ensemble ... a disc which could effectively bridge the commercial and progressive markets, and appeal to both'. But without any airplay nor TV broadcast of the track's promotional film made in Basing Street Studios, 'Downtown' achieved even less exposure than its predecessor and also died a death. According to Overend, it was one of their worst efforts, and though he had fronted the band on it, Mick admitted it was 'pretty naff'. Ian had not wanted to sing it, and though they were desperate for a hit, to him, it was no more than an ordinary cover of an ordinary song. It might've been fortuitous that such a lightweight – albeit perfectly pleasant – single wasn't the one to begin their chart career. Even so, around that time, Mick acknowledged in *NME* that Mott yearned to be a really well-established group, 'and I think a successful single is the only way'.

Meanwhile, after considering doing an album of cover versions, they returned to Basing Street Studios in August to record another collection of original material, with the working title *AC/DC*, 'because really we're just as schizoid as ever'. Sessions had begun in April, including '"Til I'm Gone': a song Mick wrote about the breakup of his first marriage; 'One of the Boys': co-written by Ian and Mick; Mountain's 'Long Red', and 'It'll Be Me': previously recorded by Jerry Lee Lewis and Cliff Richard among others.

After one week of relatively relaxed but unsatisfying self-produced sessions, the band invited Guy Stevens back for what would be the final time. They went in with very few songs, as they'd been touring so much and Ian never liked writing on the road.

During the sessions, Guy's unpredictability reached new heights. The group were at the studio with engineer Richard Digby-Smith, when Guy and engineer Andy Johns ran in wearing capes and masks, squirting everyone with water pistols. When they told Guy they had no material, he suggested they set fire to the studio, as that would inspire them to greater heights. A pile of chairs and assorted rubbish was set alight, and with some trepidation, Ian went to inform Chris Blackwell that his studio was on fire. Once he'd been reassured it was not the console but only the studio itself that had been damaged, he asked if it had really been necessary, and Ian answered 'Yeah'. Chris' reaction was 'Fine'. Ian was disgusted, but he knew Chris had a soft spot for Guy and would let him get away with almost anything. On a subsequent session, a senior engineer came in to tell Guy that the group were running beyond time and the studio was needed for other purposes. Guy promptly smashed a clock, screaming that he didn't care.

Fortunately, the bulk of the album took only about five days to record, with backing tracks done live and vocals added immediately afterwards, Ian getting progressively more croaky. Guy had unveiled a case of wine; they all got drunk, set the sound levels, chased each other around the studio while they were recording, and left the tapes rolling. One session only came to a stop when Dale collapsed unconscious into his drums.

Brain Capers (1971)

Personnel:

Ian Hunter: lead vocals, piano, rhythm guitar

Mick Ralphs: vocals, lead guitar
Overend Watts: bass, backing vocals
Verden Allen: organ, backing vocals
Dale Griffin: drums, backing vocals
Additional personnel:
Jim Price: trumpet
Guy Stevens: piano
Producer: Guy Stevens
Engineer: Andy Johns
Studio: Island Studios, London, August-September 1971
Release date: November 1971
Chart placing: UK: - US: -
Running time: 38:03
Side One: 1. Death May Be Your Santa Claus (Hunter / Allen) 2. Your Own Backyard
(Dion DiMucci, Tony Fasce) 3. Darkness, Darkness (Jesse Colin Young) 4. The
Journey (Hunter)
Side Two: 5. Sweet Angeline (Hunter) 6. Second Love (Allen) 7. The Moon Upstairs
(Hunter / Ralphs) 8. The Wheel Of The Quivering Meat Conception (Hunter / Guy
Stevens)
Bonus tracks: Angel Air (2003)
9. Midnight Lady (Hunter / Ralphs) 10. The Journey (Hunter)

Ian said that *Brain Capers* was 'five days of chaos' to him, and when he
listened to it many years later, he could hear the Sex Pistols loud and clear.
Mick called it his favourite Mott album. Overend said that after they'd
recorded it, they thought it was just a mess until journalist Lester Bangs
listened to it and said it was the one that everybody had been waiting for.

After the original titles 'A Duck Can Swim With Me' and 'How Long',
Guy renamed the opening track to 'Death May Be Your Santa Claus':
taken from an obscure arthouse film and soundtrack album by the group
Second Hand. 30 seconds of drumming explodes into a dense guitar-and-
organ-driven number, with Verden's chords and riff, Ian's lyrics, and the
repeated chorus line 'I don't care what the people may say', that sounds
more like Johnny Rotten than Ian Hunter.

Two covers with a strong anti-drugs theme followed. Dion's 'Your Own
Backyard' found Ian pursuing a mid-1960s Dylan furrow, and Mick a West
Coast feel on The Youngbloods' 'Darkness, Darkness'. Guy had suggested
both numbers, which – in view of his increasing drug problems – could've
been taken as a case of 'Physician, heal thyself'.

'The Journey' brings side one to an almost apocalyptic end. Ian's nine-minute epic of introspection began life as a poem about a bridge at London's Archway known as Suicide Bridge. Much of it was a ballad, but with an intense instrumental section and a crescendo towards the end. Verden – whose Al-Kooper-like organ fills contributed much of the atmosphere – said it was one of his favourites, and they used to play it live on a regular basis, apologising for its length, until they dropped it from the set. A version recorded earlier with mainly acoustic guitars and swirling Hammond was generally judged as technically superior but lacked the intensity of the take that Guy coaxed out of them. Almost one minute longer, it was added as a bonus track to the Angel Air reissue.

'Sweet Angeline' – originally called 'Indian City Queen' – was another of Ian's straightforward rockers, with Mick and Verden giving it their all on guitar and organ. Ian and Dale – unhappy with the rushed job they made of it – pleaded for them to try it again but were outvoted. It did, however, become a live favourite, and remained thus (as simply 'Angeline') into Ian's solo career.

'Second Love' – Verden's first completed solo composition – was a yearning ballad about a Jewish girlfriend whose second love was her religion. Verden originally sang it but passed it to Ian, admitting that his own effort was terrible. Mick's 'The Moon Upstairs' started life as a country-rocker, inspired somewhat by The Band's 'The Weight'. But Ian turned it into another punk-style anthem before its time, with a refrain of 'We ain't bleedin' you/We ain't feedin' you/But you're too fuckin' slow'.

Next came 'The Wheel Of The Quivering Meat Conception' – an 80-second fragment from an end-of-session jam that developed from an alternate version of 'The Journey': salvaged by Guy and named after a line from Jack Kerouac's lengthy poem Mexico City Blues (242 Choruses).

The album was released in a sleeve with white lettering on a scarlet background (inspired by supermarket packaging), with initial copies containing a black mask to wear while listening and a photo collage of bomber planes. It received excellent reviews. In retrospect, group members and critics look on it as something of a punk album long before its time, and it has been hailed as one of the great lost rock classics of the era. Ian claimed it sold more copies than *Wildlife*, but being released in a period where there was no shortage of exceptionally good albums hitting the high street, *Brain Capers* proved to be Mott's sole Island release that failed to reach the charts.

After the sessions were complete, the group played a concert at La Taverne de l'Olympia in Paris, filmed for French TV. It wasn't a gig or even a venue they liked, as Ian said he thought the French never understood their music. But he admitted it wasn't their fault, 'as French radio banned everything but Johnny Hallyday, who was a really good actor but a lousy singer'.

Most of October was taken up with an extensive British tour, with Paul Rodgers' new trio Peace as support. There had never been any rivalry between Paul and Mott, although the temporarily-disbanded Free had been Island Records' star act with a single and album both at number 2 in the British charts in the long hot summer of 1970.

Paul and Mick became good friends on the road – a camaraderie that would soon bear fruit, while Ian considered asking Paul to join Mott as vocalist so he could revert to keyboards and backing vocals and concentrate more on songwriting. Ian also wanted to expand the group with female backing singers and a brass section for live work: an idea received with a marked lack of enthusiasm by most of the others. As for the former suggestion, while Overend agreed that Paul was amazing, he told Ian that it wasn't the right direction for them. '*You* are the singer!', he told Ian, to which Ian responded that Paul was the best singer in the world. Overend argued that great musicians and singers didn't matter – 'It was the sum of the five people in Mott The Hoople that counted'. While Ian sometimes gave the impression of being domineering, Overend said the fact they had to talk Ian into remaining as lead vocalist against his inclinations surely indicated the opposite.

In December, the band undertook a short tour of Germany supporting Grand Funk Railroad. The experience was horrific, crossing the border to East Germany with searchlights, machine guns, razor wire and other grim reminders of the situation that had existed since the war. There were also encounters with hostile East German Cold War guards, taunting them with impressions of pop stars, while using AK47 guns as guitars.

On 30 December – relieved to be back in England – they played a fourth and final *In Concert* for BBC Radio 1 at the Paris Theatre. Eleven tracks were performed, four of them from *Brain Capers*.

Measured in terms of reputation, positive press coverage and live drawing power, Mott The Hoople ended 1971 as one of Britain's top groups. But the fates still conspired against them, as neither their singles nor albums were yet punching their weight in the respective charts.

Chapter Three: 1972

The new year had to be one of make or break, and it turned out to be both, but not in that order. The band felt increasingly burned out by January, selling meagre album quantities, increasingly desperate for that hit single, and heavily in debt with the increasing touring costs. Island Records were also losing patience. Mott felt they were a bad fit for the label, and Chris Blackwell didn't really seem interested in them. Ian thought he was their 'cut-price Dylan' competing against iconic Island singers like Paul Rodgers and Steve Winwood, and had it not been for Guy Stevens' support, he suspected the band would probably have long since been dropped from the roster.

The management called them to a meeting to say they owed too much money and would have to cut back on their tour lighting and PA. They replied that all they had was their live following, and if they had to downsize to that extent, they might as well pack it in. Nobody could agree on the financial situation – Dale thought that by this time, the Island accounts showed their albums were in profit, while the others were convinced they were not covering recording costs, and, as producer, Guy was taking half their royalties, such as there were. They *were* selling-out venues everywhere but still losing money hand over fist: a situation that could not continue indefinitely.

Though now at a low ebb, they persevered with another recording session at Island in January – taping three tracks from which another single would be chosen – with Steve Winwood's elder brother Muff as executive producer. With two tracks shelved (later to be re-recorded), 'Movin' On' was the prime single candidate. Written and sung by Mick – in open tuning, 'because it restricts you to basics and you can't go wandering off on to posh chords' – it was about the rigours of touring and his fear of flying. Despite the less-than-rosy subject matter, like 'Downtown', it was uncharacteristically cheerful and poppy with a radio-friendly chorus. But they were dissatisfied with the results and gave it to labelmates Hackensack, who, towards the end of the year, released a brutal, hard-rocking version as the only single of their brief career: also produced by Muff Winwood.

Mott's perception of the session might've been coloured by the fact that Ian disliked Muff – probably because he represented Island management and was thus perceived as having no more than a reluctant interest in the group. But there might've been another reason, in that Steve and his band

Traffic – always regarded as the jewel in Blackwell's Island crown – had just released *The Low Spark of High-Heeled Boys*. Mott suspected the title track was an unsubtle dig at them – something Steve answered with a non-committal smile when one Mott member asked him directly.

Around that time, Ian told a music journalist that the group were looking for songs. Soon afterwards, a box arrived at Island with a note suggesting the song on the enclosed tape might be suitable for them. It contained 'Suffragette City' – a new unrecorded song by David Bowie, who had released records on several different labels since the mid-1960s, but so far had only troubled the charts with one solitary top-10 single in 1969: 'Space Oddity'.

They left the tape in the box while further touring ensued, starting with a gig at Glasgow's Kelvin Hall Arena. Scheduled for April was Mott The Hoople's Rock and Roll Circus tour, with fifteen shows featuring Hackensack, knife throwers and veteran music hall comedian Max Wall. The origins of the tour idea have been lost to time but are thought to have been loosely inspired by The Rolling Stones' similar venture of the same title that had been filmed but kept under wraps and was suspected lost until its 1996 TV premiere.

Before that, Mott were booked to play two gigs in Switzerland, which meant a lengthy round-trip. Both shows proved to be a disaster, the second one being at 'Youth Centre, Berne', according to the Island booking agency. It turned out to be a concert hall that had been converted from a former gas supply reservoir. They were exhausted, had an argument on stage, and all came independently to the conclusion that they'd simply had enough. Deciding they would split, they went to the cinema. Then they took the train back to England and got drunk, laughing and joking about what to do next, finding it a very relaxed journey because all the tension had gone. Incidentally, they later learned that Escher – the artist whose name they'd helped to make famous after using one of his graphics on the first album sleeve – died that same week, aged 73.

Back in London, they had a meeting with Chris Blackwell in his flat at the Island building. When they confirmed the rumours that they were disbanding, he told them he'd spent several thousand pounds setting up the Circus tour. They could walk away if they wanted, but if they did, he would personally ensure that none of them would ever do anything in the music business again. They immediately changed their minds and promised to do it with a sense of relief. Why finish, they asked themselves, after they had struggled so hard?

Meanwhile, Overend listened to 'Suffragette City'. He was already a huge fan of the writer, loved the song, and played the tape to Ian, who liked it but was not certain it would be the hit they needed to stay in business. Ringing David to thank him, the bassist told him about the impending split and all their woes. It turned out that David had the Mott albums, was a serious fan, and told them they had to keep going: 'Leave it with me for a while'.

Overend accordingly arranged a meeting with David, his wife Angie and David's manager Tony DeFries. Afterwards, David played him part of 'All The Young Dudes' on acoustic guitar. Overend thought it was wonderful, and a meeting was fixed with the entire band. David's one-man performance knocked them all out, and they were interested in Tony's offer to extricate them from Island Records and arrange a new contract with CBS. Dale could hardly believe their good fortune, saying that David was crazy to give the song to them. David asked them to consider recording it anyway and then disband if they really must.

Buoyed by the prospect of a new beginning, they fulfilled all Rock and Roll Circus dates in April as arranged. At some shows, Ian soundly berated audiences for giving Max Wall a hostile reception.

In May, they quietly entered Olympic Studios with David Bowie as producer, ensuring that Chris Blackwell didn't find out. Tony DeFries negotiated their severance with Island, who were probably relieved to see the back of them, and merely accepted retention of their publishing as part of the deal. DeFries had originally offered David Bowie to Columbia/CBS, who rejected him, and the singer went to RCA instead. Now DeFries took Mott The Hoople to the former, who were pleased to sign them at once. In retrospect, it was a wise move. Free biographer David Clayton opined that Island 'suffocated its bands by controlling them completely'. Mott broke away from the label and reaped the benefit for a couple of years.

'All The Young Dudes' and Ian and Mick's 'One of the Boys' were recorded in two six-hour sessions. When David said *their* song had to be the single, Ian told him he must be joking. It did, however, end up as the B-side of what would be the album's only British 45. When David said that he thought 'All The Young Dudes' went on too long at the end and risked becoming boring, Ian promptly ad-libbed a rap section on the fadeout against the chorus – based partly on an impromptu heckling he'd delivered at a kid in the audience at a recent show. 'Hey you, down there with the glasses' was a one-liner taken from *The Billy*

Cotton Band Show: a staple of 1950s and 1960s radio. Immediately before the fade, Ian's barbs 'I've wanted to do this for years' (in other words, have a hit) and 'How do you feel, sick?' were apparently directed at Island Records.

Once both tracks were recorded, David Bowie suggested they ought to complete an album and asked if they had any more songs ready. Though he had several more himself just in case, he listened to what the band had, and agreed that they were great. As Ian said, David's arrival gave them 'a resurgence of energy', and everyone agreed that their new work was their best to date. A bright new dawn was beckoning.

All The Young Dudes (1972)

Personnel:

Ian Hunter: lead vocals, rhythm guitar, piano

Mick Ralphs: vocals, lead guitar

Overend Watts: bass, backing vocals

Verden Allen: organ, backing vocals

Dale Griffin: drums, backing vocals

Additional personnel:

David Bowie: saxophones, guitar, backing vocals

Mick Ronson: strings and brass arrangement

Producer: David Bowie

Engineer: Andy Johns

Studios: Olympic and Trident, London, May-July 1972

Release date: 8 September 1972

Chart placings: UK: 21, US: 89

Running time: 40:47

Side One: 1. Sweet Jane (Lou Reed) 2. Momma's Little Jewel (Hunter / Watts) 3. All The Young Dudes (David Bowie) 4. Sucker (Hunter / Ralphs / Watts) 5. Jerkin' Crocus (Hunter)

Side Two: 1. One Of The Boys (Hunter / Ralphs) 2. Soft Ground (Allen) 3. Ready For Love/After Lights (Ralphs) 4. Sea Diver (Hunter)

Bonus tracks, 2006

10. One of the Boys (Demo) (Hunter / Ralphs) 11. Black Scorpio (Demo of 'Momma's Little Jewel') (Hunter / Watts) 12. Ride On The Sun (Demo of 'Sea Diver') (Hunter) 13. One Of The Boys (UK single) (Hunter / Ralphs) 14. All The Young Dudes (Bowie, Hunter vocal) (David Bowie) 15. Sucker (Live at Hammersmith Odeon, 1973) (Hunter / Ralphs / Watts) 16. Sweet Jane (Live at Hammersmith Odeon, 1973) (Lou Reed)

David Bowie's appearance had given the group an instant shot in the collective arm, and the result was an album that left their intriguing-but-sometimes-erratic Island work in the shade. As Ian was later to remark, he gave the title track real energy, and as great as the original song was, he thought David's version was too fey. The only other non-original number – the opener 'Sweet Jane' – reportedly startled Lou Reed himself when he heard how fast Mott performed it, though he later admitted he really liked what they had done to it.

Ian really hits his stride with a selection of snarling Rolling Stones-like rockers. The Overend co-write 'Momma's Little Jewel' – complete with fluffed start – has a barbed lyric evidently addressing a girl 'just outta school, fresh from the nuns that made you'. Mick's guitar break and David's sax add colour towards the finish, culminating in a sudden ending of the master tape. 'Sucker' (a Mick and Overend collaboration) and 'Jerkin' Crocus' (with a guitar intro echoed in ELO's 'Ma-Ma-Ma Belle' and The Stones' 'Dance Little Sister') are in similar territory – the kind of venomous, swaggering pieces that always seemed just out of reach on previous Mott albums; David's sax unobtrusively complementing the guitar and organ lines without dominating proceedings.

Side two opener 'One Of The Boys' builds subtly from a quiet guitar intro, forging ahead with the same three chords that would later warm the pot for 'Can't Get Enough', to say nothing of the intro's old-style telephone dialling: recurring after a false fade and chorus return. 'One Of The Boys' also appeared on the B-side of 'All The Young Dudes', and an edited version became the follow-up single in America, Canada and Germany.

Written and sung by Verden, the out-of-character 'Soft Ground' was, by his own admission, a subtle comment on what was going on between the other band members. He speaks the lyrics rather than sings, with suitably eerie organ sounds alongside David's backing vocals and what Verden called his 'freakish guitar'. Pete called it the best song on the album, admitting it was 'not very Mottish', but the most futuristic number they'd ever done. Mick's medley of 'Ready for Love' and the instrumental coda 'After Lights' brings a more dreamy flavour to proceedings.

The album closes with Ian's reflective ballad 'Sea Diver' – a song about the trauma of songwriting itself, and a yearning to 'escape this iron veil'. His subdued piano chords and Mick Ronson's tender string arrangement bring the album to a poignant conclusion.

The initially-intended front cover design was a black and white photograph of a small boy waving a cardboard cut-out guitar on a playground in Regent's Park Estate, London. It was rejected in favour of an image from an old sombre-hued American tailoring advertisement showing three sharp-dressed dudes. Ian thought it very classy, while Dale dismissed it as boring.

All in all, David Bowie's supervision had given the band an album that for the first time sounded like a proper production. On the previous four, Guy Stevens had played the role of trying to encourage and coax ideas out of them, but not being a musician himself, he never contributed anything tangible. On *All The Young Dudes*, the sound is far more confident, more rounded and much richer, while the songs sound properly crafted and less a case of *roll the tape, see what happens and it'll do.*

A minor hiccup on the single had to be remedied when the BBC ruled that a reference to stealing clothes from 'Marks and Sparks' (Marks & Spencer department stores) contravened their policy around having brand names in songs, on the grounds that it was advertising. But a ban was circumvented by substituting the phrase with 'unmarked cars'. (Mentions of shoplifting and suicide, the latter coming in the opening line, were evidently acceptable.)

The song completely turned Mott The Hoople's career around. Mick admitted that David Bowie producing it for them was the best thing that ever happened. Ian was always grateful and even surprised that Bowie even took an interest in them. Who else at that stage in his career – Ian asked many years later – would start giving away time and songs to other people like Iggy Pop and Lou Reed, bearing in mind that, until the summer of 1972, he was still a one-hit-wonder, attempting to re-establish himself? Although very ambitious himself, he 'still found time to do other things as well, which I think is quite remarkable'.

Released at the end of July, the single entered the chart at 22 and peaked at 3. Suddenly the group were on the Radio 1 playlist, appeared on *Top of the Pops* again (three times in August) and had that long-awaited hit. The album followed on 8 September, again to ecstatic reviews, peaking at 21 in a four-week run. The following month, Island responded with an eight-track compilation album *Rock'n'Roll Queen*, featuring a sleeve design by Philip Castle, based on a Marilyn Monroe image. Compiled by Muff Winwood, the album included 'Midnight Lady' and material from the first three albums, emphasising the more aggressive songs. Ian commented that they had 'all the favourites on there', and was alarmed that it might outsell the first CBS album, but the compilation never charted.

Over September and October, they undertook a British tour, supported by Home. In mid-October, they spent a day demoing three songs – 'Hymn For The Dudes', Verden's 'Nightmare', and an early version of 'Honaloochie Boogie', which Ian said was 'about being on the streets of Northampton with no money about, and then a kid turns you on to rock and roll'. Honaloochie was a name he dreamed up that he thought looked good when written down.

Next on the schedule was an American tour. Most of the setlist was drawn from the new album, adding 'Midnight Lady' and 'Angeline'. At a Tower Theatre, Philadelphia show, David Bowie introduced the band and later joined them for two encores. While on tour, Ian kept a diary that formed the basis of his book *Diary of a Rock'n'Roll Star*: published to great acclaim two years later. Another show – at Memphis' Ellis Auditorium – ended with Joe Walsh jamming with the band. Afterwards, Ian, Verden and Joe got very drunk, and just for a laugh, decided to go and look at Elvis Presley's house Graceland: uninvited, as if they were merely tourists visiting a stately home. As soon as they were seen on the security cameras, they were politely asked to leave.

'All The Young Dudes' peaked at 37 in the American singles chart in November, the album at 89. The follow-up single 'One Of The Boys', with 'Sucker' on the B-side, reached only 96 early the following year.

The group returned to London on Christmas Eve. A few days later, David Bowie telephoned Ian to ask if they could have a meeting about the future. After an unproductive evening with David at his place in Beckenham, Ian realised that their association was over. Though it was never formalised or even really discussed, it was evident to all that neither party really needed the other. Nevertheless, David had already told Ian that he should lead the group. For the previous three years, it had been a fairly democratic affair with Ian and Mick the joint leaders. Ian had gradually become the more prolific songwriter, the main vocalist, the frontman, and, with his striking appearance, the face of Mott The Hoople. Moreover, from a management point of view, sometimes policy decisions required speedy action to be taken. If nobody took responsibility, and they had to discuss it first, it inevitably slowed things down. Within less than twelve months, two other Mott members would leave and be replaced.

Chapter Four: 1973

When Ian broke it to the rest of the group that he was assuming the mantle of leadership, their reaction was inevitably mixed. Dale seemed ready to accept what he said. While they had started as five equals, the balance shifted when David Bowie and Tony DeFries entered the picture and when Ian got out from behind the piano to become the frontman with a guitar. Everybody knew his face and image: the hair, omnipresent shades and that distinctive Maltese cross-shaped guitar. Who would the fans remember most, Ralphs or Hunter? They all talked about it, and it met with their explicit approval.

But the storm clouds were not long in gathering. Verden was increasingly at odds with the other four, wanting them to record more of his compositions, and insisting on a more prominent role on stage and in the studio. Tensions increased, and in January, after a couple of rows onstage at gigs, Verden announced he was leaving. In the past, when he'd threatened to walk out, Mick had told him to calm down and everything would be alright. But Mick too had finally had enough, and this time his response was 'When do you want to go?'

Overend was saddest to see him depart, having respected him as probably the best musician of them all, the joker of the group and always good for a laugh until he began writing songs and wanting to be taken more seriously. Ian said that Verden wanted to change their sound completely, into 'a combination of Black Sabbath and Lou Reed', which was just not Mott. Over the next few years, Verden made several solo singles and an album, worked with various other bands but never hit the same heights as Mott The Hoople. Ian said that once Verden left, Mick 'kind of left mentally as well'.

In hindsight, there was an analogy between their situation and that of The Beatles and The Stones. In the case of the former, from 1967 onwards, Paul McCartney gradually became *de facto* frontman, with John Lennon starting to consider a life and career outside the group. With The Stones, a precarious balance between the ever-sparring Mick Jagger and Keith Richards wobbled badly at times but continued to endure.

Mott The Hoople were now a four-piece. Having lost one member and put an end to any further involvement with Bowie and DeFries, they feared CBS might be getting cold feet. Ian panicked and thought a solo career could be beckoning: an idea that made Dale particularly angry. But when Ian asked all three whether they'd like to play on his first single, they agreed to with some reluctance, on the grounds that they had nothing better to do.

Going into AIR Studios, they recorded a new faster version of 'Honaloochie Boogie' – with altered lyrics ('Wanna tell Chuck Berry the news'), Andy Mackay on sax, and Paul Buckmaster on cello: echoing Ian's love of the Roy Wood sound – and 'The Ballad Of Mott The Hoople': a wistful soul-baring number about their disbanding the previous March. Ian remarked that the recordings sounded 'very Mottish' and should be issued as such. Recording more new songs, Overend and Dale asked Ian if this was his solo album, to which he retorted sharply: *no*, it was *their* album.

After a period where the group's future hovered in the balance, they were on track once more, with a new management company – H&H Enterprises, headed by Fred Heller in New York and Bob Hirschman in London. A second CBS album was recorded from February to April at AIR studio two and Abbey Road. At AIR, Roxy Music were simultaneously recording their second album *For Your Pleasure*.

Ian had always been an admirer of The Move and Wizzard, and loved their 'See My Baby Jive', which was on its way to number 1 at the time. So Ian's first choice for Mott's next producer was Roy Wood, but he was too busy at the time. Overend wasn't keen on the idea, as he thought Wizzard's records sounded too messy with the automatic double-tracking, so he suggested asking either John Lennon or Mike Leander. However, after Roxy Music's Andy Mackay and Brian Eno listened to 'Honaloochie Boogie', they told Mott they didn't need a producer and should do it themselves.

By the beginning of May 1973, the second CBS album was complete. It had been ten months since the previous single, and 'Honaloochie Boogie' was chosen as the next. Featuring Andy Mackay on sax and Paul Buckmaster on cello, it was released in May, returning Mott to *Top of the Pops* and peaking at number 12. The B-side 'Rose' was another Ian ballad, but in light of the fact that all Mott members were contributing to songs and arrangements, he began a policy of giving each member a share in the composing credits.

Released on 20 July, the album was simply named *Mott* – in a move meant to establish and consolidate the group's name.

Mott (1973)

Personnel:
Ian Hunter: lead vocals, rhythm guitar, piano, harmonica
Mick Ralphs: vocals, lead guitar, organ, Moogotron, mandolin

Overend Watts: bass, backing vocals
Dale Griffin: drums, backing vocals
Producer: Mott The Hoople
Engineers: Alan Harris, Bill Price, Jon Leckie
Additional personnel:
Paul Buckmaster: electric cello
Morgan Fisher: piano, synthesizer, backing vocals
Mick Hince: bells
Andy Mackay: tenor saxophone
Graham Preskett: violin
Thunderthighs (Karen Friedman, Dari Lalou, Casey Synge): backing vocals
Studios: AIR and Abbey Road, London, December 1972-April 1973
Release date: 20 July 1973
Chart placings: UK: 7, US: 35
Running time: 39:09
Side One: 1. All The Way From Memphis (Hunter) 2. Whizz Kid (Hunter) 3. Hymn For The Dudes (Hunter / Allen) 4. Honaloochie Boogie (Hunter) 5. Violence (Hunter / Ralphs)
Side Two: 6. Drivin' Sister (Hunter / Ralphs) 7. Ballad Of Mott The Hoople (26th March 1972, Zurich) (Hunter / Griffin / Watts / Allen) 8. I'm a Cadillac/El Camino Dolo Roso (Ralphs) 9. I Wish I Was Your Mother (Hunter)
Bonus tracks 2006
10. Rose (Hunter / Watts / Griffin) 11. Honaloochie Boogie (Demo) (Hunter)
12. Nightmare (Demo) (Allen) 13. Drivin' Sister (Live 1973, Hammersmith Odeon) (Hunter / Ralphs)

Maybe by accident, maybe by design – this was more or less a concept album about the highs and lows of a rock group on the road, becoming disillusioned, exhausted, seeing dreams of stardom crushed underfoot, yet still getting a buzz out of living the life. Every track but one was written or co-written by Ian. 'All The Way From Memphis' referred partly to the event at the Ellis Auditorium gig, in December 1972, of forgetting the 'six-string razor', when Mick's guitar was inadvertently shipped to the wrong state for the next gig, and partly to the excesses of rock stars who may forget they're ordinary mortals after all: 'you look like a star, but you're still on the dole'. The striking piano intro echoed Ian's admiration for the style of Leon Russell. The track climaxed with Andy Mackay's sax and Mick's guitar echoing and responding to each other in fine style. Saxophonist Bobby Keys – noted for his work with The Rolling Stones

– originally played on the session, but they 'caught him on an off day', and his contribution was scrapped. Once it was complete, Ian was not satisfied with the mix. He said it was 'an album track' to him, emphatically not wanting it put out as a 45, and told Dick Asher, the head of CBS. The moment their backs were turned and they went on the next American tour, Ian's instructions were ignored. As he conceded, sometimes he was a pretty bad judge of his own work. An edited version was released, giving Mott their second top-10 single, peaking at ten at the end of September.

'Whizz Kid' – a more subdued song with intriguing synthesizer and guitar from Mick – told of a girl from Brooklyn Heights who had the aura of a star about her, despite a difficult background. 'Hymn For The Dudes' was a slow, stately number that fused Rachmaninoff-style piano with Ian singing against an acoustic guitar, before the great musical build, aided by Thunderthighs on backing vocals, and Ian's voice dropping almost to a whisper on the line 'You ain't the nazz, you're just a buzz, some kinda temporary' – Mick's guitar solo then cutting in and sending it to new heights.

The first of two Ian-and-Mick collaborations – 'Violence' – started as a parody of the group's regularly-recurring frustrations, but during the sessions, Ian and Mick genuinely came to blows. Filled with interesting little embellishments – Graham Preskett's manic violins (violins = violence); a guitar lick from Cat Stevens' 'Matthew and Son', and Mick's two-note police siren effect played on organ – the increasingly aggressive street-punk delivery eventually breaks into a fight ('Me and you/Get your coat off'), before the fisticuff exchanges fade out and the frenzied violin-led outro appears for another manic burst before the final fade. Ian said afterwards that if the mock punch-up had continued for another quarter of an hour, they would've had 'the real thing'. Not surprisingly, Mick afterwards went on record as having hated the album because of the bad memories.

'Drivin' Sister' – inspired by a car journey Ian had with Guy Stevens – was a kind of homage to Stones-style swagger and raunch, intercut with a car starting and accelerating, its horn blaring as it pans from one stereo channel to the other, and, at the end of the song, the driver getting out and walking along the street. It segued into 'Ballad Of Mott The Hoople (26th March 1972, Zurich)' – a mournful postscript to the group's story up to the split the previous year. Ian refers to changing his name in search of fame and how they shed their illusions on the rocky road to stardom, learning a thing or two: 'Rock 'n' roll's a loser's game/It mesmerises and I can't explain'. Rarely if ever has a lyricist so-well captured the ambivalence of being in a group with its helter-skelter ups and downs in one song of four verses.

'I'm a Cadillac/El Camino Dolo Roso' gives Mick his final chance to shine on a Mott album. It's a bright and airy song about cars that flows into an acoustic instrumental and is one of only two Mott songs throughout their recording career that didn't feature Ian.

Finally, 'I Wish I Was Your Mother' was an achingly personal Ian ballad about – as he admitted – his jealousy of people who had had really good childhoods. Its subdued air was enhanced through mandolin and bells that were lying around the studio.

The British release had two different covers. The first pressing comprised a gatefold with the head of Michelangelo's David printed on an acetate sheet through which a collage of group pictures could be seen. The D. H. Lawrence poem 'A Sane Revolution' was printed on the back above the track listing and credits on a fading-white-to-pink background. The lyrics were on the inner bag. Later pressings had a single sleeve with the head of David on a white card. Much to the band's annoyance, Columbia in America rejected the British artwork in favour of a lacklustre band photo on a brown background, and with the back cover's Lawrence poem removed.

Critics and fans hailed *Mott*, and have always regarded it as their best and most consistent work. In Britain, it was their only top-10 album, peaking at 7 in a 15-week run. Ian said that sound-wise, it was the result of 'When we figured out what to do in the studio'. As for the lyrics, he later explained to biographer Campbell Devine that he was trying to get across that rock was not about 'superstars and God in the sky'. There were losers and winners, and Mott was a very honest band. Basically, his message was 'Wait a minute, this is how it really is'.

Meanwhile, after recording the album as a quartet with guest musicians and Ian and Mick contributing keyboards, the band were augmented by two additional keyboard players for a three-week American tour in July and August. Morgan Fisher, formerly of late-1960s pop favourites The Love Affair and then Smile (a pre-Queen group including Tim Staffell, who was replaced by Freddie Mercury), was also one of the first British musicians to acquire a synthesizer. The second, Mick Bolton, was a quiet, unassuming player who'd been with a couple of little-known bands. Morgan's prog-rock band Morgan had recently folded, and he was thinking of giving up the music business altogether. Yet he kept his eyes on the *Melody Maker* adverts, and the next major vacancy to catch his eye led to Mott. He had seen them live once, about a year previously, and the only thing that impressed him was Overend's hair. Nevertheless, he joined, initially as a stand-in, and only then did he realise what a powerful act they really were.

Mick Bolton remained as a temporary guest musician but left at the end of the year to become a Jehovah's Witness, while Morgan was subsequently confirmed as Verden's replacement and a full group member. More ominously, at the end of August, when they returned from the first leg of their American tour, Mick Ralphs left, playing his last gig with Mott in Washington on 19 August. His dissatisfaction had been building for some time, becoming exacerbated after Verden walked out. With personal differences – and the feeling that some of his songs weren't really suited to either his or Ian's voice – he became increasingly uncomfortable in the group and with the new post-Bowie musical direction. While the album was being made, Mick regularly talked to Paul Rodgers, who was left without a group now that Free had split, reformed, recruited additional musicians to replace two departing core members to fulfil contractual commitments on tour and in the studio, and then finally collapsed. The more rugged blues-rock style so close to Paul's heart gradually made Mick realise that his musical direction lay along that path.

Ian had always regarded Mick as one of the best guitarists around and was genuinely saddened that he wanted to move on. He was so keen to keep him in the group that he offered him half his royalties on a co-writer basis, even though Mick was writing about an eighth of what Ian was contributing. But it was to no avail – they could no longer work comfortably together, and Mick realised that a new band with Paul Rodgers would be the way ahead. Having told the others that he intended to leave, Mick agreed to stay on and fulfil all existing commitments, including the tour, until a replacement guitarist could be confirmed.

After Mick had gone, Ian acknowledged that the making of *Mott* had been difficult for Mick, who didn't like the songs and would come in a couple of hours late and merely put his guitar parts down. He complained about Ian playing 'all these chords', and suggested he kept it more simple. Ian said he couldn't do it that way, because if they did, 'Nobody in the band can sing it simple', so Mick went off and found himself a singer. 'He couldn't have really picked a better one, could he?'. It was perhaps a coincidence that the singer Mick chose was the one that

Ian had seriously suggested trying to recruit for Mott The Hoople about eighteen months earlier.

Morgan had always known that Mick was bound to leave sooner or later, especially when he told them he'd started jamming with the remaining two members of the now non-existent Free. Just for fun, Morgan went to a session in the country, where he jammed with Paul, Mick and the drummer Simon Kirke. He made the mistake of taking his synthesizer along and felt afterwards that they were slightly put off by that. Even so, he never doubted that the move to what would become Bad Company was perfect for Mott's former guitarist.

Several big-name guitarists were discussed. Among them were Mick Ronson – particularly as David Bowie had just announced (what would turn out to be a temporary) retirement from live work, Zal Cleminson from The Sensational Alex Harvey Band, and Ray Major from Hackensack. Ian was keen to recruit an American guitarist such as Joe Walsh, Ronnie Montrose or Leslie West, but Overend told him that Mott was an English band and was going to stay one. Ian's old friend Miller Anderson was in the frame for a while, but their close affinity alone would've only exacerbated group friction. In the end, they chose former Spooky Tooth guitarist Luther Grosvenor, whom they'd known from their days on Island. He was asked to adopt the alias of Ariel Bender: a name that Lynsey de Paul originally thought up for fun for Mick Ralphs.

The new lineup immediately spent a week rehearsing a two-hour set at Emerson, Lake & Palmer's Manticore Studios in Fulham. Dale thought Ariel was good at playing Mick's solos note for note, but he had to be told exactly what to play. Even making allowances for the fact that he'd just joined, the sound and feel were not quite right. It was strange because Luther (Ariel) was considered among the ten top British guitarists when he was in Spooky Tooth, but once he joined Mott, it seemed as if his creativity was completely stifled. Sometimes he just had the wrong ideas completely. When Ian asked him to put a solo on 'Trudi's Song', Luther played something that sounded like Jimi Hendrix, which was not at all what the writer had in mind.

The next stop for the group was another appearance on *Top of the Pops*, doing 'All The Way From Memphis'. They then flew back to resume the American dates, which included two nights at Winterland, San Francisco, supported by Joe Walsh and Bachman-Turner Overdrive – or, according to Morgan Fisher, Bachman-Turner Overweight. Another night to remember was on the *Midnight Special* TV show, where they shared billing with The Rolling Stones.

While on the other side of the Atlantic, Mott nearly had to deal with another lineup change. On their arrival at some of the hotels, the receptionist greeted them with a message for Mr. Peter Watts to phone Peter Grant urgently. Mick was in the process of forming Bad Company with Paul Rodgers, and their first choice for bassist was Overend. Grant – Led Zeppelin's manager – was also looking after Bad Company, and though hesitating to say no to the formidable Mr. Grant, Overend told him that he intended to remain where he was.

Their return home coincided with the release of a new single recorded during one of their last sessions with Mick. 'Roll Away The Stone' – with a guitar intro that some remarked paid homage to The Beatles' 'While My Guitar Gently Weeps' – was another of Ian's songs, which saw them back on *Top of the Pops* in the coveted new release slot. Mott said that each appearance on the show was 'absolute hell – always a day of grind and misery' with endless waiting around. But it helped them to sell more records (the 'Midnight Lady' experience being an exception) and was a necessary evil. Augmented with girl-trio Thunderthighs on backing vocals, a short dialogue section before the final choruses, and two sax players, a smiling Tony Blackburn (well known at the time for not being a Mott fan and not being afraid to admit it on air) introduced the song as 'Roll Away The *Stones*'. A twelve-week chart run saw it peak at number 8 and qualify for a silver disc, and with record sales always being better at Christmas than during summer, it even outsold the higher-charting 'All The Young Dudes'. After penning three top-20 singles for the group that year, Ian walked excitedly into the office of their publicist Tony Brainsby, telling everyone that he'd 'cracked it' and now had the knack of writing hit records at will.

In Britain, 1973 would go down as the year that glam rock was at its zenith, with Slade, T. Rex, Sweet, Wizzard and the later infamous Gary Glitter rarely far from the charts or TV every Thursday night. Mott The Hoople were also part of the scene, if only through association (not to mention Overend's head and chest hair sprayed with silver paint, his platform boots and silver swallow-shaped bass guitar, making him a rival for Slade's equally-conspicuous guitarist Dave Hill). Yet they were clearly on what might be called the art-rock spectrum alongside Bowie and Roxy Music. Ian had always seen Mott as 'flash rock' like The Stones, but after the Bowie connection and 'All The Young Dudes' Mott were pigeonholed as glam. It was one of the factors that made Mick realise he was at odds with their style. Dressing up might have been stupid, but everyone is allowed a little stupidity when they're young. Some four decades on, rock critics could look back on Mott The Hoople and take a more measured view of their place in music history, underlining the difference between them and their peers. While they were enshrined in the collective imagination as glam rockers, Alexis Petridis noted in *The Guardian*, with its lyrical dismissal of the Beatles, "All the Young Dudes' was the song that definitively drew a line between the '60s and the '70s, but there was always something noticeably earthier about Mott The Hoople, than their glittery contemporaries'. Simon Kirke of Bad Company called Mott a zany band: 'The Monty Pythons of rock'.

Morgan Fisher summed them up in greater depth, giving Ian due credit for his skills as a lyricist who always wrote 'with balance, humanity and sensitivity', even calling him 'Britain's Bob Dylan'. Glam rock, he opined, was 'disposable', but Mott's music was serious, because of their front man's songwriting. 'The band should have given his lyrics more attention, but we didn't care – we just got on and gave the best musical support that we could.'

The year ended in a blaze of glory, with a British tour that was almost fully sold out, and received a sheaf of positive reviews. During the show at Oxford New Theatre, they were presented with a silver disc for sales of the *Mott* album. Supporting them were Queen – a new act who shared Tony Brainsby as publicist, and whose first album and single had received positive media reaction, though they'd gained no chart action as yet. The last two shows of the tour – on 14 December at Hammersmith Odeon – were recorded for a live album. They coincided with the news – announced on stage that night – that on the previous day, Dale and Paula Greaves (a well-known page-three model) had married at a registry office. Nobody else knew at the time except Ian, who'd been best man. A party was held for the couple after the final gig – guests included not only all of Mott and Queen but also David Bowie, Paul Rodgers, Mick Ralphs, Guy Stevens, Mick Jagger, Andy Mackay, Eddie Jobson and Andy Williams.

When not rehearsing or playing, Ian was making plans for the next project. They'd just recorded a demo for the next single – 'The Golden Age Of Rock 'n' Roll' – at Olympic Studios, and he was talking about the forthcoming album to be recorded in January 1974. Provisionally called *Weekend*, it would be more aggressive than the last, built around the story of a group of British kids, their experiences and lifestyle over a typical weekend. By the time Mott began rehearsing it at Advision Studios, it had become *The Bash Street Kids,* until the DC Thomson publishing company – who held the copyright to the *Beano* cartoon strip feature of the same name – withheld permission. The song Ian had written around the title became 'Crash Street Kidds', the concept was modified, and the album – the follow-up to *Mott* – became *The Hoople*. Overend quipped that maybe it should've been the second part of a trilogy: *Mott, The* and *Hoople*.

Chapter Five: 1974

After a very successful 1973, Mott entered the new year bursting with activity, ready to record a new album for release by February and then tour Europe after that. However, the sessions proved to be a troubled time for all. They planned to record at AIR Studios again, but finding the studio to be fully booked, settled for Advision instead. Recordings done there were mixed and overdubbed at AIR, but only after Dale – now responsible for production to a greater extent than any of the others – realised that the Advision tapes sounded faulty and that shortcomings with the AIR tape machines were affecting sound quality. The group wanted to scrap the Advision material and start again at AIR, but management and record executives told them to mix the album as it was.

Moreover, they'd come to realise that guitarist Ariel fitted in well on stage, but proved to be less than fully engaged when it came to the studio. At one point, Ian went to America without giving the others a reason; only a terse order to 'Sort Bender out'. When he returned, he found they'd completed an Overend song – 'Born Late '58' – with the writer on lead vocals, 12-string and rhythm guitars, and according to the album insert credits, Manfred Mann's bass guitar, with Ariel playing slide. Fortunately, Ian was pleased with the results. Apart from Mick's 'I'm a Cadillac/El Camino Dolo Roso', it would be the only track the group ever recorded and released without Ian's involvement.

Another matter that didn't help was the British three-day week that the government had called during a national miners' strike, thus causing problems within the power industry and creating the ever-present risk of a power cut: something that happened several times throughout the sessions. To some, it was as if the country was descending into industrial and economic chaos, with Ian telling the press the whole country had gone back to the Middle Ages in a week. Meanwhile, Overend had an encounter one evening with a car park attendant who was angry with him for owning 'a huge flash car', and it nearly ended in a punch-up.

Andy Mackay (credited this time as Jock McPherson) and Howie Casey were brought in to play saxophones. Howie asked to be left off the credits as he was an experienced session musician of the old school and thought Andy was a dreadful player of the modern avant-garde school – Howie not wanting people thinking it was him playing badly.

Ian was still hugely inspired by the sound of Roy Wood and Wizzard and arranged the songs with plenty of sax, cello and keyboards. It gave the skills of Morgan Fisher – confirmed as a full group member at the end of the previous year – a higher profile. Mick Ralphs had moved on from Mott but remained a close friend and associate. He returned for their *Top of the Pops* appearance doing 'Roll Away The Stone' – appropriately enough, as he had played on the recording, though his solo was removed and Ariel added his own – note for note – to the album version. Mick also returned to play some guitar parts on the new album, resulting in Ariel's instrument being turned down in the mix and sometimes appearing as basically playing rhythm. Morgan later said he was pleased to contribute to what he called 'the musical broadening' of the band and that the ever-perceptive Ian called him 'the icing on the cake'. Even so, in retrospect, he could see why many people preferred 'the raw early Mott', singling out *Brain Capers* as 'stunning'.

The Hoople – born of so much trouble – was released on 22 March, with the single 'The Golden Age Of Rock 'n' Roll' appearing one week earlier. That was another recording illustrating its writer's homage to the sound of Wizzard and Phil Spector, featuring heavy use of backing vocals and sax, and a brief spoken radio-DJ intro mimicking American DJ Alan Freed. The song had a sting in its tail – the last verse taking a swipe at Leeds City Council – 'You 96-decibel freaks' – who had tried to impose a 96-decibel noise limit on local rock concerts to protect fans from possible hearing loss. John Peel – who when not broadcasting for the less-mainstream listener on Radio 1 in the evenings, also wrote a weekly column in and reviewed new singles for *Sounds* – welcomed Ian's being prepared to aim a few slings and arrows in his lyrics at those 'melancholy persons who feel that rock music should be rendered at a volume comparable to that of a mouse farting in a jewellery box'. 'The Golden Age Of Rock 'n' Roll' peaked at number 16 in a seven-week run, four places below the record that gave birth to the genre: Bill Haley & His Comets' 'Rock Around The Clock' – which had just been reissued to coincide with a British tour by the veteran rock 'n' rollers.

Little did Mott know, but they'd had their last top-20 entry. Although the song sizzled with excitement and remained one of Ian's regular live staples, he later called it an average song that should not have been put out as a single – and Overend said that he could not 'bear it'.

The Hoople (1974)

Personnel:

Ian Hunter: lead vocals, rhythm guitar, piano

Ariel Bender: guitar, backing vocals
Overend Watts: bass, 12-string guitar, backing vocals
Dale Griffin: drums, backing vocals
Morgan Fisher: keyboards, synthesizer
Additional personnel:
Howie Casey: tenor saxophone
Jock McPherson (Andy Mackay): saxophones
Mike Hurwitz: cello
Lynsey de Paul: backing vocals
Mick Ralphs: guitar, backing vocals
Graham Preskett: violin, tubular bells
Blue Weaver, Sue Glover, Sunny Leslie, Barry St. John, Thunderthighs: backing vocals
Producer: Mott The Hoople
Studios: Advision and AIR, London, January-February 1974
Release date: 22 March 1974
Chart placings: UK: 11, US: 28
Running time: 43:00
Side One: 1. The Golden Age Of Rock 'n' Roll (Hunter) 2. Marionette (Hunter) 3. Alice (Hunter) 4. Crash Street Kidds (Hunter)
Side Two: 1. Born Late '58 (Watts) 2. Trudi's Song (Hunter) 3. Pearl 'n' Roy (England) (Hunter) 4. Through The Looking Glass (Hunter) 5. Roll Away The Stone (Hunter)
Bonus tracks, 2006
10. Where Do You All Come From (Hunter / Ralphs / Watts / Griffin) 11. Rest In Peace (Hunter) 12. Foxy, Foxy (Hunter) 13. (Do You Remember) The Saturday Gigs (Hunter) 14. The Saturday Kids (Hunter) 15. Lounge Lizzard (Hunter) 16. American Pie/The Golden Age Of Rock 'n' Roll (Live 1974, Broadway) (McLean / Hunter)

Topped and tailed with two hit singles, *The Hoople* found its creators veering between introspection and anger. 'Marionette' is undoubtedly the masterpiece, and Ian hailed it as the best track they'd ever done. Not so much a song, it was more a mini-operatic epic with echoes of Gilbert and Sullivan, and excerpts of dialogue that inspired the up-and-coming Queen in birthing 'Bohemian Rhapsody' the following year, as Freddie Mercury admitted. (That track may also owe more than a little to 10cc's 'Une Nuit A Paris': from their 1975 album *The Original Soundtrack*). Alternately laced with black humour, cynicism and a kind of Gothic horror, 'Marionette' tells in five minutes the tale of a character who sees he's become no more than a marionette, manipulated and tormented by his audience. The ambitious production – for which Dale was largely responsible – included saxophone, cello, violin, and a chorus of 'Voix grotesques à la Quasimodo' from Ian, Ariel and Overend. Ariel also supplied the lunatic laughter halfway through, and Overend hit him repeatedly over the head with a tin tray to produce the crashing sound on the choruses: much to the fury of a studio tea lady when she saw the state of the tray afterwards.

The mid-tempo 'Alice' was Ian's song about a New York prostitute on 42nd Street, with Lynsey de Paul on a 'whistling Moog mouse', Morgan on organ and synths, and Overend on bass played through a Leslie speaker. 'Crash Street Kidds' – a sequel to 'Violence' – was inspired by Ian's dislike of new towns and their seeming lack of heart or centre. A brutal number, it told of a disaffected street gang that decided to form their own private army and take over the country – ending with Ian going down in a hail of machine-gun fire.

Written by Overend with a little uncredited lyrical help from Mick, 'Born Late '58' is about going out on the town with a girl below the age of consent: the title suggesting a 1958-model car. Ian had been encouraging Overend to write, especially after Mick had left, and later said the song was potential single material, though Overend thought it fell short in the lyric department and lacked a decent hook.

'Trudi's Song' is Ian's love song to his wife. It's a simple number with Morgan's piano played through a Leslie cabinet. Dale thought it would've belonged more on an Ian solo project.

There was no such tenderness on the next track, which finds Ian going for the jugular over the state of the country. 'Pearl 'n' Roy (England)' points a finger at the failings of and subsequent disillusionment with contemporary politicians. 'Hi number 10/How's things going?' is presumably a reference to Edward Heath: occupant of 10 Downing Street when the song was recorded. Before the album came out, Conservative Prime Minister Heath was ousted in the subsequent general election – albeit by a very narrow margin – after which Labour opposition-leader Harold Wilson replaced him at the head of a minority government. Opening with a noisy saloon bar scene, it later becomes a punk-ish sing-along with a clear Roy-Wood-influenced sax line and a taunt at the ruling class of 'Amateurs, shamateurs, bullshit calamitors!'

'Through The Looking Glass', with its unobtrusive strings arranged by Graham Preskett, is another introspective and largely solo-Ian song, with a stream-of-consciousness lyric where he contemplates his reflection. An alternative version laden with Ian's ending expletives was made in order to panic company executives into thinking it was the finished version. As it was only intended for private circulation, Ian was annoyed when twenty years later, it was unearthed and issued on a compilation without his consent.

The Hoople concluded with a slightly altered version of 'Roll Away The Stone' – using the original backing track but with Ariel's lead guitar line replacing Mick's, and Lynsey de Paul voicing the spoken section.

The album cover was a colourised portrait of Kari-Ann Muller, who was already known for having appeared on the sleeve of the first Roxy Music album. This time, multiple portraits of the four Mott members' faces (excluding Morgan, who was not yet a full member) were in her hair. A sleeve insert included the lyrics.

On release, the record was praised for its 'uncomfortable aura, as if the group was finding the studio claustrophobic and longing to escape'. One reviewer applauded Ian's 'new punk-poet imagery', saying it established Mott as Britain's major new band: which *must*'ve amused them, as it was the seventh record in their five-year history. Mildly less successful than their last British album, *The Hoople* fell just short of the top 10 in a five-week stay, but in America charted higher than its predecessor. In hindsight, though, Ian would admit that it was 'The beginning of the end'.

The rest of the spring was taken up with a 45-concert tour of America and Canada, with Queen initially supporting them, until Brian May was sidelined with hepatitis. Mott The Hoople was now a six-piece for live work, with Blue Weaver – formerly of Amen Corner and The Strawbs – augmenting them on organ in place of Mick Bolton. To finish the tour, there was a week of sold-out concerts at New York's Uris Centre, making Mott the first rock group to pull off such an achievement on Broadway. The setlist consisted mostly of material from the CBS/Columbia albums, opening with Ian intoning a fragment of Don McLean's 'American Pie', ending with 'the day the music died – or did it?' as a prelude to 'The Golden Age of Rock 'n' Roll'. At the Broadway shows, life-size marionettes and smaller puppets were lowered or moved on to the stage during 'Marionette', with two of them pushing Ian into a crouching position as he sang 'Oh God, these wires are so tight' towards the end.

On the first night, the group wondered whether this boldly innovative idea had been a mistake. Ian looked out at the audience and thought they were all heavy-duty business people in their forties at least, who'd come expecting a Broadway show, not a rock group. Fortunately, they were still receptive, but the group were relieved when younger punters eventually came, and the rest of the week went really well. One show was recorded for a forthcoming live album.

One of the few sour moments came backstage before their Broadway debut when three-quarters of Led Zeppelin arrived after a very good liquid lunch, and John Bonham insisted he wanted to play on the encore of 'All The Young Dudes'. He said she had it on the jukebox at home, his son regularly played it, and he knew it inside out. As he would not take no for an answer, a scuffle broke out, Dale was kicked, and afterwards, Zeppelin's manager Peter Grant apologised to Ian. Some said it was the only time Grant had ever been known to say sorry to anybody.

The Beach Boys' Mike Love also came to the Uris to see one show and was apparently offended that the Mott members never said hello to him. Afterwards, Dale said nobody would've expected to see one of The Beach Boys at a Mott gig.

American record sales were brisk during the tour, with *The Hoople* reaching the top 30 and out charting *Mott*'s showing the previous year, while the Island compilation *Rock'n'Roll Queen* was released in May and reached a modest 112. 'The Golden Age Of Rock 'n' Roll' became their third and final American hit, reaching 96.

While the group were in America, Ian made his debut as an author back at home when Panther published *Diary of a Rock'n'Roll Star*. He originally wanted to call it *Rock'n'Roll Sweepstakes*, but the publisher thought the new title would render it more saleable. Based on jottings he made on the American tour in November and December 1972, it was one of the first books that could be called a rock memoir. Up to then, a few songwriters had dabbled in literature – notably John Lennon, Bob Dylan, Marc Bolan and Alan Hull – but Ian's was far removed from their comic essays, cartoons, verse and stream-of-consciousness prose. As well as recounting the ups and downs of being a busy band on the road, Ian's book included the funny stories of how he bought his iconic Maltese-cross-shaped guitar in a San Francisco shop and of that surreal night when some of them went to Graceland and breached security to enter Elvis's mansion, only to be informed politely by a maid that Mr. Presley was tired and not seeing anybody. There are also a couple of thoughtful pages about the creative processes of songcraft – from writing something new and convincing the band that it's good enough to work on, to then arranging, producing, mixing and cutting it to become the finished article on record. By turns humorous, vitriolic, self-deprecating, informative and always down to earth, *Diary Of A Rock'n'Roll Star* garnered advance orders of around 50,000, deservedly positive reviews, and went into several reprints. Some 20 years later, it was acclaimed as something of a modern classic and reissued.

The group returned to England on 3 June. On the flight from New York, Ian saw Eric Clapton, and as they were leaving the plane, asked if he'd like to join Mott. It was a friendly exchange and Eric complimented him on the book, but the invitation never came to anything. The group had, however, realised that Ariel was not a good musical fit, and the search was on for a new guitarist. At around the time they finished recording *The Hoople*, he told Martin Hayman of *Sounds* that he hated rehearsing with the band: 'You come out of the studios where it all sounds great, and then you try and put it together as a set, and it sounds like rubbish'. He was not the first musician to have it forcibly brought home to him that what could be magically embellished in a state-of-the-art studio might not sound quite as good in a rehearsal or live situation.

A few days later, 'Foxy, Foxy' – recorded during *The Hoople* sessions and produced by Ian, Overend and Dale – was released as a single. Some of the music weeklies were ecstatic, *Disc and Music Echo* calling it their best ever. Being a softer, more Phil-Spector-sounding number, none of the group really shared Ian's enthusiasm for it. Overend called it a good song, but not really Mott material. It received limited airplay, and despite another *Top of the Pops* appearance, only peaked at 33 in a five-week chart run and was not released in America. To Dale, it demonstrated that Mott were really a touring and albums band, but now they were expected to deliver a potential hit single every two months, and they couldn't.

On 5 July, Mott headlined at the Buxton Festival, Derbyshire, sharing a bill with Lindisfarne and Man. Although it was an unseasonably cold and wet day – leaving them wondering for a moment whether they dare go on with fierce winds blowing rain into the microphones – they still went down well. Likewise, they triumphed the following day at the Douglas Lido, Isle of Man. In hindsight, some observers thought Ian's heavy emphasis on the 'American Pie' segment at the start of the show as he sang 'The day the music died', seemed prescient.

These turned out to be not just Ariel's last live dates with the group, but also their final British ones altogether for 35 years. Another was planned for the London Music Festival at Alexandra Palace on 31 July but cancelled. The ill-fated 'Foxy, Foxy' received one more outing when they played a Dutch TV pop show, and that concluded Ariel's stint with the band. After that, they went briefly into the studio to work on a few new tracks, including 'Colwater High' – which Ian thought would make a good single – and 'One Fine Day'. However, the group seemed to lose motivation for a while, and the tracks were not completed.

Meanwhile, Dale undertook production duties on the Hammersmith and Broadway recordings at AIR and Trident. Initial plans to release a double album were aborted for technical reasons, although, thanks to the wonders of digital technology, a double CD finally resulted 30 years later.

Group and management were planning further recordings, and dates at home and abroad were scheduled for the next year or so. Before this could take place, a new guitarist had to be recruited. In September, it was announced that Ariel had left amicably, and Mick Ronson (dubbed 'Ricky Monsoon' by the wags at *NME*) would replace him. A new single, 'Saturday Gig', was to be released on the eve of an extensive tour of Europe and Britain.

In theory, Mick Ronson was the ideal recruit. He'd been interested in replacing Mick Ralphs the previous year after David Bowie disbanded The Spiders From Mars, but managerial issues between MainMan and H&H had put paid to the idea. Ronson then embarked on a relatively successful solo career, but felt uncomfortable as frontman, realising he was more suited to being a band member. Ian was thoroughly fired up by what looked like a new lease of life for Mott, the band having been chastened by the relative failure of a single most of them disliked anyway.

Prior to that, the group had come close to disbanding. Dale later said they 'more or less broke up' in August when 'Foxy, Foxy' failed. He tried to persuade a rather disinterested Ian that they ought to record a 'proper single', said he'd convinced CBS that they had a really great song, and obtained some studio time. He then persuaded Overend and Morgan to record what he confessed later was a 'ghastly' song he'd written – 'Sunset Summer Nights' – and a backing track was made with Howie Casey on sax. The rest of them waxed enthusiastic over this substandard number, while Ian looked increasingly uncomfortable. Once Dale had put a guide vocal on it, Ian said he also had an idea for a song, beckoning them to the piano, and playing them the first version of a work in progress called 'Saturday Kids'. Later, he revealed that he thought they all reckoned he might leave, so Dale concocted the idea to get Ian into the studio, play him their horrible song, he would then hate it and come up with something really worthwhile. The plan succeeded. Ariel played a solo on it, but it was his last chance and 'he blew it'.

The next month, Mott were up and running again, with Mick Ronson on guitar and all guns blazing. A demo of 'Saturday Kids' had been recorded as a marathon ballad lasting over six minutes. They reworked it, with Ian rewriting the lyric until it became less of a semi-autobiographical rites-of-passage song. The new version focused more on the band's history from 1969 to the present, with references to damaged seats at the Royal Albert Hall, the 1972 split and the Broadway triumph, closing with a muted refrain of 'Goodbye' repeated several times. The fade was shorter, the sax playing removed, and the more concise 'Saturday Gig' emerged, lasting just under four minutes. Mick added extra guitar, and they recorded Ian's medium-paced song 'Lounge Lizzard' – the only one that had been started and completed with Mick Ronson's involvement. Both tracks were scheduled for the next single. Then, while they were in the studio, Ian turned to Dale and said they were not using 'Lounge Lizzard' after all, as he intended to withhold it. Would Dale 'knock something together out of the live material' instead? An angry Dale held his tongue, and with the aid of engineer Bill Price, cobbled together a segue of 'Jerkin' Crocus', 'Violence' and 'One Of The Boys': deliberately badly-edited as 'a two-finger job' at Ian.

On 10 October, Mott began a 19-date tour of Europe, with Anglo-Norwegian band Titanic as support. At the first show – Olympen, Lund, Sweden – they were greeted ecstatically with scenes reminiscent of Beatlemania at its height: fans swamping the stage and streets outside the venue. The gig went really well, and afterwards, the band and road crew had a very convivial meal seated around a large table.

In spite of a great opening night, all was not well within the camp. Ian sensed that the old camaraderie was missing. He was sure that recruiting a musician and arranger of Mick Ronson's calibre would be the shot in the arm that the ailing group badly needed, but it was not working. Overend and Dale seemed to resent Ronson's presence, sitting apart from him at breakfast on tour. As the next newest member, Morgan didn't seem unduly concerned at first but slowly gravitated towards Overend and Dale, who'd been the group's backbone since they were Silence. They felt it had become the Hunter-Ronson Band with a rhythm section.

There was the suspicion that Mick's management had seen his joining the band as a way to boost his profile and help plug his solo material by showcasing some of his repertoire on stage. Overend also believed his management had suggested a change of image by telling the bassist to discard the thigh-length boots, dress in a blue boiler suit and cut his hair short, so he ended up without an image at all. Everyone – including Ian in dark denim – looked dowdy except for Mick: resplendent in a sparkling white jumpsuit that made him really stand out under the stage lights. He reckoned it was obvious who the real star of the show was meant to be. Roger Taylor of Queen once said Mott were 'hod-carriers in gilt': a comment they never really cared for. By the time of the tour, glam rock had become passé, and Mott were as ready as everyone else to discard the bright clothes, heels and long hair to become a normal-looking rock band again.

Stan Tippins – who remained an invaluable helping hand and judge – felt from the start of the tour that the new combination was not right. He thought they sounded terribly weak from his vantage point at the front of the audience. Mick Ronson did not come through forcefully, perhaps because he was ill-at-ease at being the new member, perhaps because of the personality problems behind the scenes. To make matters worse, he and Ian were warned that tickets for the British dates were not selling as well as expected. Overend also admitted they didn't sound great on stage, and everybody sensed that Mick was uncomfortable.

On 18 October – less than halfway through the tour – the single was released in Britain as 'Saturday Gig' – or so the label read, though press adverts made it 'Saturday Gigs', which is what the group were plainly singing. (It also appeared in Germany, the Netherlands, Yugoslavia and New Zealand. But only in the latter country did the label say 'Saturday Gigs'). If the media had expected a hard-hitting rocker after the downbeat 'Foxy, Foxy', they were disappointed. The group recorded a slot for *Top of the Pops*, but it was never shown. Capital Radio gave it an enthusiastic reception, placing it at number two in their chart, but Radio 1 were less impressed: a three-week national chart run, peaking at 41 being the best they could manage. Overend echoed the group's view that it was one of the best records they'd ever made – 'a lovely, nostalgic number' – and they'd set their sights on a return to the top 10. The single's disappointing performance was a crippling blow to general morale.

The now-complete live album was imminent, though the band seemed unexcited by the prospect. Ian told the press that Dale had finished it and it sounded fine to him, but admitted the two had grown so far apart by this time that Dale 'just did the whole thing'. Ian was sick of the songs, as he'd sung them so many times, and with a shrug, he accepted that phoney applause had to be dubbed in, as some of the live mic's had not been working. He said the album was probably not coming out in Britain anyway, as there seemed to be a much stronger demand for it in America: 'We'll see what happens with it later on'. Columbia had rejected any idea of the double album they'd wanted, also turned down the suggestion of a bonus 10" record, and initially wanted it to be American-only.

Nevertheless, it was given a worldwide release on 1 November, two days before the final European show – at the Concertgebouw, Amsterdam – and the band's return home. The single album was a compromise that left them less than contented, with an indifferent track selection including only two hit singles, two B-sides and nothing from *The Hoople*. In particular, the exclusion of 'Marionette' rendered the rear-sleeve shot of the band onstage with the lifesize puppets (probably the high point of the whole performance) as rather pointless. Initial British pressings came with a foldout souvenir handbill, while the American copy included an inner bag with black and white photos and liner notes.

Live (1974)

Personnel:
Ian Hunter: lead vocals, rhythm guitar
Ariel Bender: guitar, backing vocals
Overend Watts: bass, backing vocals
Dale Griffin: drums, backing vocals
Morgan Fisher: piano, backing vocals
Additional personnel:
Blue Weaver: organ (US)
Mick Bolton: organ (UK)
Stan Tippins: backing vocals
Producer: Dale 'Buffin' Griffin
Recorded at Hammersmith Odeon, 14 December 1973; Uris Theatre, Broadway, NY, 8 and 9 May 1974.
Release date: 1 November 1974
Chart placings: UK: 32, US: 23
Running time: 53:48
Side One (Broadway): 1. All The Way From Memphis (Hunter) 2. Sucker (Hunter / Ralphs / Watts) 3. Rest In Peace (Hunter) 4. All The Young Dudes (David Bowie) 5. Walkin' With A Mountain (Hunter)
Side Two (Hammersmith): 1. Sweet Angeline (Hunter) 2. Rose (Hunter / Watts / Griffin) 3. Jerkin' Crocus / One of the Boys / Rock And Roll Queen / Get Back /

Whole Lotta Shakin' Goin' On / Violence (Sunny David / Hunter / John Lennon / Paul McCartney / Ralphs / Dave Williams)

A 30th-anniversary two-CD edition in 2004 comprised 23 tracks, with six songs featured twice, either in their entirety or as parts of medleys. Both records started with 45 seconds of a taped excerpt from Holst's *The Planets* as the band walked on stage.

Though financial constraints had put paid to the concept of a proper double album with two sides for Hammersmith and two for Broadway, with so many glaring omissions, the result was the best it could've been under the circumstances. Some groups would release live albums of reasonably faithful renditions of the studio versions, while others took the opportunity to give tried-and-trusted favourites a complete makeover. Mott followed the former path.

The two ballads are performed sensitively, particularly with Morgan's exquisite classical piano introduction on 'Rose', creating some dynamic contrast against the rock 'n' roll. Ian works up a sweat on 'All The Way From Memphis', and with Ariel's guitar-playing approaching sheer frenzy, one hardly misses the saxophone. Two tracks from the old Island days – 'Walkin' With A Mountain' (which had to be shorn of a part of Ariel's solo because of time constraints) and 'Sweet Angeline' – have an energy that Guy Stevens never managed to capture on the original studio versions. Ian delivers some between-number banter before the medley on the Hammersmith side: 'We hope you're gonna get your arses up, 'cause it's been a bit nippy of late'. The medley – merging four original numbers with bursts of 'Get Back' and 'Whole Lotta Shakin' Goin' On' – threatens to descend into a train wreck, but somehow holds together. At times, his voice sounds perilously shot. On the vinyl version of 'Walkin' With A Mountain', his vocal is partly submerged in the sheer wall of sound, but on the remastered CD version, he can be clearly heard straining for the high notes, singing flat in places or merely declaiming the lyrics instead of trying to sing. Other groups would've probably dubbed on a new vocal after the fact. Mott were content to let it go, warts and all.

American journalists loved the album, one calling it 'a scorcher', and another saying that the 15-minute medley was 'as close to the spirit of Little Richard as anyone could hope to be in 1974'. In Britain, reviewers were less impressed, with *NME* proclaiming, 'Whole Lotta Nothin' Goin' On'. Significantly, *Live* charted lower in Britain than America, where it became and would remain their only top-30 entry.

About halfway through the European tour, things began to go seriously wrong. Several German dates were cancelled at short notice. At one stage, the rest of the tour was going to be pulled, but in the end, the last two dates – at Paris and Amsterdam – were saved. By then, the fragile threads holding the group together were coming apart. They had become two camps: Ian and Mick in one, the remaining three in the other. They mostly travelled separately, and the atmosphere was increasingly frosty between Ian and Dale. At one point, Ian approached Paul Thompson of Roxy Music to ask if he was interested in taking over on drums, the implication being that if he accepted, Dale would be sacked. Mick Ronson was dismayed to find that the act he'd joined with such high hopes just a few weeks before now seemed to be at war with itself – saying he was 'getting disgusted by the behaviour of the band'. At first, they had welcomed him with open arms. Now, it was as if everyone but Ian strongly resented his presence. The image on the rear sleeve of the debut album, a reptile eating its own tail, had become a self-fulfilling prophecy.

Morgan had been as ready to accept Mick as anyone, even though his arrival had happened suddenly without any full band discussion. He was the only one without previous experience of working with the new guitarist. But Ian, Overend and Dale had all done so successfully during the making of the first CBS single and album. They even changed their hairstyles and wardrobe as soon as Mick joined: a sure sign they were prepared for major changes. Unfortunately, they didn't have enough rehearsal time before playing live, and Morgan was convinced that Mick privately told Ian that he had 'got to get away from these guys'.

Though nobody knew at the time, the Amsterdam show turned out to be Mott's swan song. A 29-date tour of Britain – opening at Glasgow Apollo on 10 November and closing at the same venue on 20 December, with Sailor as support – had been arranged. Sessions were booked at AIR in January to begin the next album – provisionally called *Showtime* – though Ian had little new material apart from 'Lounge Lizzard': the shelved B-side that never was. Meanwhile, Ian made what was planned as a short business trip to America, staying at manager Fred Heller's house in New Jersey. A day or two later, press reports revealed that during dinner one evening, Ian collapsed and was rushed to hospital, where he was diagnosed with physical exhaustion and was ordered to take five days of complete rest.

The first four tour dates – all in Scotland and all sold out – were rescheduled for late December, with an initial date to be at Leeds on 15

November. One week later, Mott's British management representative Bob Hirschman confirmed that the tour had been scratched but would be rescheduled for 1975, subject to their itinerary and the state of Ian's health. Over 50,000 tickets had been sold, and the group were expected to lose a five-figure sum through the postponement. Even so, Ian was now under doctor's orders to take two months of complete rest, as any attempt to fulfil existing commitments could lead to permanent health issues.

The next few weeks brought various, sometimes conflicting, rumours about the group's future. There was speculation they were going to disband, but not until after farewell American and British tours and a final studio album. Next, it was reported that Ian had arrived back in Britain earlier than expected and was in London recording a solo album to be co-produced by Mick Ronson, who was also playing on the sessions. They planned to complete the project before starting on the group's farewell album early in the new year. Official sources continued to deny any split until after Christmas when it was at last confirmed that both Ian and Mick had left the band. It was also reported that CBS had offered Ian $750,000 for a solo deal – something he furiously denied, threatening to sue any journalist or publication that persisted in saying so. In a brief statement, he said that after five years, he'd had enough, and the group had gone as far as it could.

With hindsight, it gradually became apparent that the group had been almost in its death throes since the summer – demoralised by an inability to build on its brief period of success and torn apart by personality conflicts. Recruiting a musician of the calibre of Mick Ronson had been the solution that instead became the straw that broke the camel's back. Ian Hunter had carried the responsibility of leading, doing nearly all the press and writing most of the songs – and it was a heavy load. He was gutted that Mick – whom he thought to be the only guitarist available who could save them after an increasingly difficult few months – had not been given a fair chance to make everything work, and Ian was at the end of his tether.

Above: An early publicity picture of Mott The Hoople. Ian Hunter soon dispensed with the moustache. (*Mike Hale*)

Right: Ian, one of rock's elder statesmen, still maintaining an extensive schedule of recording and live work in 2008. (*Croydon Music Library*)

Left: *Mott The Hoople*. The debut album design was based on a colourised reproduction of 'Reptiles' by M.C. Escher, 1969. (*Island/Universal Music Group*)

Right: *Mad Shadows*. Not a human face, but a mirror image of a smoking fire grate, 1970. (*Island/Universal Music Group*)

Left: *Wildlife*. The photoshoot for the album they later nicknamed 'Mildlife' took place at Carlton Bank, Cleveland Hills, North Yorkshire, 1971. (*Island/ Universal Music Group*)

Right: *Brain Capers.* 'Five days of chaos,' Ian called the work now regarded as a punk album before its time, 1971. (*Island/Universal Music Group*)

Left: *All the Young Dudes.* The design, by David Bowie's friend George Underwood, was based on an American tailor's advert, 1972. (*Sony Music*)

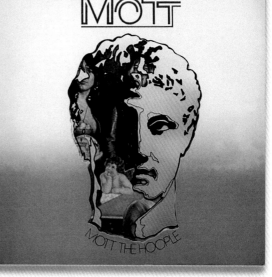

Right: *Mott.* The initial gatefold sleeve, featuring a Michelangelo image printed on an acetate sheet with a collage underneath, 1973. (*Sony Music*)

Above: Mott The Hoople and their first producer Guy Stevens, who said there were only two Phil Spectors – and he was one of them. (*Croydon Music Library*)

Above: Mott in 1971, a major live attraction but still trying hard for that elusive major hit single. (*Croydon Music Library*)

RELEASED MARCH 19 · NOW READ ON...
THE END
OF OUR TALE IS THE BEGINNING OF MOTT'S NEW ALBUM · WILDLIFE · ILPS 9144

Left: One of a series of similar music press adverts for *Wildlife*, March 1971.

Above: 'Seventy-three was a jamboree, We were the dudes and the dudes were we, did you see the suits and the platform boots?' (*Croydon Music Library*)

Above: Mott backstage, augmented by Mick Bolton (left) as a second keyboard player on tour in 1973. (*Davidson Rockpix*)

Right: Ian fronting Mott on TV for a performance on 'Roll Away the Stone', 1973.

Left: Ian and three-quarters of Queen, with producer Roy Thomas Baker (right), plus Trudi Hunter and Barbara Baker (front) in 1977. (*Mike Hale*)

Right: Pete Watts, who early in his career became better-known by the traditional family second forename, Overend. (*Mike Hale*)

Left: Mott with new guitarist, formerly Luther Grosvenor (back) of Spooky Tooth, now renamed Ariel Bender in 1973. (*Croydon Music Library*)

Right: Mott with Morgan Fisher in his distinctive keyboard jacket (front), 1974. (*Davidson Rockpix*)

Left: Mott on stage on Broadway, New York, performing 'Marionette' as Ian tries to ward off the giant puppets, 1974. (*Croydon Music Library*)

Right: The sheet music for 'Saturday Gig', the 'lovely, nostalgic number' which they expected to become a Top ten single. It peaked at 41. (*April Music Ltd*)

Left: *The Hoople*. Model Kari-Ann Muller with stars in her hair on what would be Mott's last studio album in 1974. (*Sony Music*)

Right: *Live*. The group's farewell album, and the only one to chart higher in America than at home, 1974. (*Sony Music*)

Left: *Ian Hunter*. The eponymous debut solo album, co-produced by Ian and Mick Ronson, with an Escher-inspired design by Mark Springett, 1975. (*Sony Music*)

Right: *Drive On.* The first of two albums with Nigel Benjamin (centre) and Ray Major (second from right) replacing Hunter and Ronson in the renamed outfit, 1975. (*Sony Music*)

Left: *All-American Alien Boy.* Ian found renewed inspiration after moving to the US, but later called the result 'commercial suicide', 1976. (*Sony Music*)

Right: *Shouting and Pointing.* Mott's last album, featuring a rock and roll battlefield design that took several weeks to assemble, 1976. (*Sony Music*)

HOOPLE: 'We gave David as much as he gave us.'

Left: Ian and Mick Ralphs rehearsing backstage in 1973.

Above: Mott leaving glam rock behind for the final chapter. Mick Ronson (front, right) joined, but the new beginning precipitated their collapse within weeks, 1974. (*Croydon Music Library*)

Left: The partnership between Ian and Mick Ronson endured, despite occasional interruptions, until Mick's death in 1993. (Mike Hale)

Right: The Nigel Benjamin-fronted Mott, ready to drive on in 1975. (*Croydon Music Library*)

Above: Mott at the time of the release of debut single 'Monte Carlo' and their first album in 1975. (*Davidson Rockpix*)

Right: Mott at Clearwell Castle, where they recorded the second album in 1976. (*Croydon Music Library*)

Left: *Ian Hunter's Overnight Angels.* Ian later called the album (dubbed 'Overweight Angels' by *NME)* the worst he'd ever done. 1977. (*Sony Music*)

Right: *World Cruise.* Featuring Steve Hyams (centre), Dale Griffin said the mini-album released in 1993 'should not have been inflicted on the public'. (*See For Miles*)

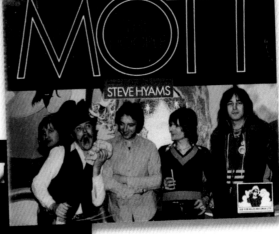

Left: *British Lions.* The debut album by the John Fiddler-fronted band, a modest US success, fared poorly in Britain, 1978. (*Vertigo/ Universal Music Group*)

Right: *Trouble With Women.* British Lions were dropped by Vertigo and RSO and then disbanded. The final album appeared a year later in 1980. (*Cherry Red/Proper Music*)

Left: *You're Never Alone With a Schizophrenic.* Ian's solo debut for Chrysalis became the only US Top 40 album of his career in 1979. (*Chrysalis/Universal Music Group*)

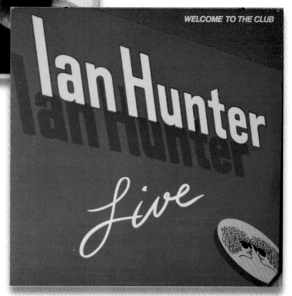

Right: *Welcome to the Club.* It was originally a double album recorded mostly live on stage in New York, 1980. (*Chrysalis/ Universal Music Group*)

Left: John Fiddler, fronting British Lions on a broadcast for Radio Bremen, Germany in 1978.

Right: A press advert for British Lions' debut album and single in 1978.

Left: John Fiddler and Ray Major onstage with British Lions during the US tour in 1978.

Right: A press advert for Mott at Sisters Club, February 1971 (note ticket price in shillings despite the adoption of decimal currency earlier that month).

SISTERS CLUB

834 SEVEN SISTERS RD., N.15 (Opp. Seven Sisters Tube)

14 mins. Oxford Circus

FRIDAY, FEBRUARY 26th   10/-   7.30 p.m.

MOTT THE HOOPLE
+ BREWERS DROOP
Lights by Parthogenenesis - Sounds by Iron Fairy
Transport: Victoria Line Tube to Seven Sisters, Liverpool Street Main Line.
Buses: 41, 241, 259, 279, 149, 67, 76

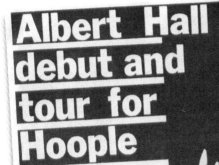

Albert Hall debut and tour for Hoople

MOTT THE HOOPLE, who return from America in mid-June, are set for a short British tour in July—and the itinerary includes a date at London's Royal Albert Hall, Mott's first appearance at the venue.

The group have a single released on Island on June 11. Titled "Road To Roam" it is an Ian Hunter composition and was recorded in New York. Producer was Shadow Morton, who was responsible for the Shangri-Las.

Dates for the tour are Pavilion, Felixstowe (July 3), Royal Albert Hall (8), Spa Royal Hall, Bridlington (16), Floral Hall, Southport (11), Town Hall, Truro (24), Guildhall, Plymouth (25), Town Hall, Cheltenham (30) and Dome, Brighton (31).

Other dates may be fixed by the Island Agency.

included a fire at their Cologne concert when three people were killed, have forced them to call the tour off.

United Artists are organising a British tour for the group in September.

MOTT THE HOOPLE: deb

Above: Mott The Hoople to appear in July 1971 at the Royal Albert Hall, where audience damage subsequently led to a ban on rock groups there.

Right: A press advert for Ian's debut solo album and British tour dates in spring 1975.

Ian Hunter
New solo album released 28 March

Hello
The weathers fine,
glad you like the single
hope you like the album
which CBS tell us is
number 69038. It's the
best we've ever done.
Love
Mott the Hoople

POST CARD

POST OFFICE PREFERRED

Bamforth

301882

PLYMOUTH PUBLIC LIBRARY
MUSIC AND DRAMA LIBRARY
DRAKE CIRCUS
PLYMOUTH PL4 8AL

Published by BAMFORTH & CO. LTD Holmfirth, Yorkshire Printed in England
No. 47 'COMIC' Series

Left: A promotional postcard (with a non-musical cartoon on reverse) for *Mott*, sent to the author's old workplace in 1973.

Right: The reunited Mott The Hoople at Hammersmith Apollo in 2009, with Mick Ralphs on guitar and Martin Chambers on drums. (*Wikimedia Commons*)

Below: Ian out front at the same gig, with Dale joining in on drums at the end. (*Wikimedia Commons*)

Chapter Six: 1975

As far as Ian Hunter was concerned, by the beginning of the new year, Mott The Hoople were finished. All he needed was a short break to recharge his batteries after the increasing stress of the last few months, to realise that there were many things he could do as a solo artist that he couldn't within the framework of a group. He had several songs waiting to be recorded, a guitarist to work with, and two months of studio time booked at AIR. Mick flew to join him in America, where he was staying in a house belonging to old friend and Blood, Sweat & Tears drummer Bobby Colomby. They worked on new material for several days, Mick then returning to England to recruit a new band. One of the first he asked was Morgan Fisher, who was, however, still furious with Mick and Ian about the split. In the end, Mick recruited Geoff Appleby (from Mick's pre-Bowie band, The Rats), Pete Arnesen (formerly keyboard player with Daddy Longlegs, Taggett and The Rubettes) and Dennis Elliott (former drummer for The Roy Young Band and If).

By the end of January, the new album was well under way. Within a few weeks, it was complete and ready for release, and the band were rehearsed for Ian's first solo tour.

Ian Hunter (1975)

Personnel:
Ian Hunter: vocals, rhythm guitar, piano, percussion
Mick Ronson: lead guitar, organ, Mellotron, harmonica, bass
Geoff Appleby: bass, backing vocals
Dennis Elliott: drums, percussion
Pete Arnesen: piano, keyboards
John Gustafson: bass
Producers: Ian Hunter, Mick Ronson
Recorded at AIR Studios, January-March 1975
Release date: 28 March 1975
Chart placings: UK: 21, US: 50
Running time: 40:38
All songs written by Hunter unless stated otherwise
(Side Two tracks 3 and 4 were indexed as one on the CD reissue)
Side One: 1. Once Bitten Twice Shy 2. Who Do You Love 3. Lounge Lizard 4. Boy (Hunter / Mick Ronson)
Side Two: 1. 3,000 Miles From Here. 2. The Truth The Whole Truth Nothin' But The

Truth 3. It Ain't Easy When You Fall 4. Shades Off 5. I Get So Excited
Bonus tracks, 30th anniversary 2005 reissue
9. Colwater High 10. One Fine Day 11. Once Bitten Twice Shy (Single version)
12. Who Do You Love (Single version) 13. Shades Off (Poem) 14. Boy (Single
version) (Hunter / Mick Ronson)

For the next phase of his career, Ian hit the ground running with the song
that would become his best-known number after leaving Mott The Hoople
– in fact, it was his only solo hit in Britain. 'Once Bitten Twice Shy' – with
its distinctive ''Allo' at the start (reverse bookending the 'goodbye' at the
end of 'Saturday Gig'), had *classic rocker* stamped all over it. In Ian's
words, it was 'a direct modernisation of Chuck Berry – just those couple
of extra chords made all the difference'. Cryptically, when asked what or
who it was about, Ian said he was 'saying something' on it, but covered
it up by using a girl character. It's an infectious song with a wonderfully
simple rhythm guitar throughout, supplemented by pub-style piano, and
to quote Charles Shaar Murray's review in *NME*: 'It smoulders away until
Ronno kicks it into overdrive with a blazing power-chord sequence that
Jimmy Page himself wouldn't have been ashamed to put his name to'. One
week after the album release, an edit of the song was issued as a single in
Britain – minus the first few seconds and faded out in the last chorus. It hit
number 14: Ian's only major British solo success. The complete version, at
almost one minute longer, is the real McCoy, with Ian working himself into
a vocal sweat against the guitar crescendo, to a proper finish. The song was
subsequently covered by Great White (whose hit 1989 version was their
only American top-ten entry), Shaun Cassidy and Status Quo.

Also edited slightly was the second single, 'Who Do You Love', though it
failed to chart. It was an equally infectious number, with boogie piano and
rasping harmonica, and was later covered by The Pointer Sisters. Next was
a re-recording of 'Lounge Lizzard' – the Mott B-side that never was (with
prominent cowbell à la 'Honky Tonk Women') – a slightly misogynistic
number about meeting young women at the Speakeasy after finishing with
his first wife Diane and before meeting Trudi.

Side one's closer 'Boy' is a slow, brooding eight-minute epic, balancing
piano, Mellotron, guitar and some neat bass runs to sheer perfection.
Ian said it was not about one particular person, but two or three, with a
little of himself in there. He later admitted that the message of despair
and encouragement was predominantly – but not completely – about
Joe Cocker.

Following the lengthy and elaborate 'Boy', '3,000 Miles From Here' is Ian unplugged – a short, sweet solo tune with just acoustic guitar, close to the mood of an early-Dylan love song. It prepares the ground well for the slow but vicious burner that is 'The Truth The Whole Truth Nothin' But The Truth' – a slow but fierce guitar song which could be an angry answer to a bad review, a retort to music industry people who'd served Ian badly, or to anybody with whom he had a score to settle.

'It Ain't Easy When You Fall' segueing into 'Shades Off' is another dramatic five-minute-plus epic. A plaintive ballad, it was long thought to have been a self-pitying song about Ian being knocked off the pedestal, but he later admitted it was really about Mick Ralphs – a man who would talk of shops, boats and planes, or in fact, anything, except getting down to business. A poignant lengthy chanting chorus approaching the grandeur of 'Hey Jude' at times fades slowly as Ian recites a five-verse poem at the end, the music cutting out sharply at the end of the last line. In the past, Ian had printed poems by Baudelaire or D. H. Lawrence on the back of album sleeves. This time, he wrote a poem of his own.

A complete change comes with another no-holds-barred rocker to finish the album. 'I Get So Excited' was so commercial that CBS briefly considered it for single release. The lead break at the end gets wilder and wilder until a simple, sudden cut is the only ending possible.

The sleeve design was a graphic illustration of Ian against a night sky with a mix of dreamlike and demonic images: notably two owls in flight facing the viewer as if poised to attack. The work of artist and musician Martin Springett, it was based on M. C. Escher's drawing 'Bond of Union'.

Of the six bonus tracks on the 2005 reissue, only two did not duplicate to some extent what was already on the record, both having been written and recorded during the final Mott The Hoople sessions. 'Colwater High' was a commercial tune with prominent piano and strong vocal harmonies. Like 'Foxy, Foxy', it suggested Ian was setting his sights on a more catchy pop direction, especially as he once had it in mind as a potential single. 'One Fine Day' showed more characteristic bite. After a piano intro, a more muscular guitar figure joined the fray, complementing a lyric of defiance:

My whole world is upside down
A lot of people want me under the ground
But I know it'll change
They'll come around one fine day

It's clearly a rehearsal take that was presumably not taken any further, as Ian says at the end that they should 'Knock the whole last instrumental bit on the head'. As the item is less than two and a half minutes long anyway, the result with excised instrumental minus any further development would've left them with an unusually short track.

Coming within only a few weeks of the group's dissolution, the album basked in general critical approval. *NME* called it 'Killersville', while *Disc and Music Echo* said it would be 'a pleasant surprise for the mourners of Mott'. It would prove to be Ian's most successful solo album in Britain – its 15-week stay peaking at 21, equalling that of *Mott* eighteen months earlier.

The album players were retained for the touring band, except for Pete Arnesen, who was in hospital for an operation. Blue Weaver – who'd just begun working with the Bee Gees – deputised for Pete on piano and organ, and the tour opened on 18 March at Exeter University, finishing at Fairfield Halls, Croydon on 6 April, with Jet as support. The set included five of the new album's tracks, alongside some Mick Ronson songs and three Mott hits – Ian not being particularly fond of 'The Golden Age of Rock 'n' Roll', but realising that, as a surefire crowd-pleaser, it had to be included. Most venues were sold out, and the press reaction was unanimously favourable.

The visit to Britain also included Ian's appearance on BBC Radio 1's *My Top Twelve*, introduced by Brian Matthew, in which Ian chose his all-time favourite tracks. Among them were Dylan's 'Like A Rolling Stone', as 'The look of him, the voice, everything about him' had made such an impact on Ian; The Rolling Stones' 'Brown Sugar', which he called 'The greatest, most amazing rock riff ever'; Lorraine Ellison's 'Stay With Me Baby': probably Ian's all-time favourite, and numbers by Little Richard, Jerry Lee Lewis, The Righteous Brothers, David Bowie and Free. When the matter of why he left the group came up in conversation, Ian said he was not yet ready to talk about it. He had no wish to cause any upset because he was sure that the memory of Mott The Hoople was still cherished by many. While still keen for success, it was a matter of 'timing and zeroing in on that point where everybody thinks the same way as you do', but he was not going to compromise with what he wrote.

When Ian and Mick returned to America, Ian planned to live and work there for the immediate future. In May, they played several dates, including the Felt Forum, New York, and the Spectrum in Philadelphia. Ian was annoyed by reports in the British music press that attendances were poor, him claiming that all venues were over three-quarters full. After they came off the road, they were offered gigs in Japan and Australia, but it came too late. Because of management difficulties resulting in payment delays to the other musicians, they had to return to England.

Ian and Mick spent the next few months writing and recording in a small basement studio. Ian was keen to record a follow-up with most if not all of the same musicians, but contractual agreements required the next project to be a Mick Ronson album. Reluctantly, they put their musical partnership on hold, Ian telling Mick that he couldn't work with him anymore as long as he remained with MainMan. They stayed friends, but for the next three years – in Ian's opinion, three lost years in which the management 'destroyed our band' – the pair pursued separate career paths.

Meanwhile, the Mott The Hoople split had left the three remaining members temporarily beached. Overend said it 'was almost like a bereavement'. Early in the new year, he began writing new songs with Blue Weaver, though without necessarily intending to form a group, but Dale was interested in being involved if that was to be the case. Soon afterwards, Blue was offered work with The Bee Gees, who were also looking for a bassist, and asked Overend. When he declined, Morgan contacted his old colleagues, and they began to coalesce once more. Having several new songs between them – the majority written by Overend – they booked sessions at Gooseberry Studios, Gerrard Street, London, with Overend on vocals, guitars and bass for the backing tracks of over twenty songs. They initially received a fan petition to retain the old group name but instead, thought of calling themselves The Hooples, before deciding on merely Mott, which seemed the most simple, and confirmed their identity and connection with the old group. It was apparent from music press reaction at the beginning of the year that to keep the full name would be unwise. Some writers said that Mott The Hoople without Ian Hunter would be like The Rolling Stones without Mick Jagger.

Two new members were needed. Hackensack guitarist Ray Smith had been their first choice when Mick Ralphs left in 1973 but was unable to join at the time for various disputed reasons. Hackensack had split a few months later and Ray was now available. As there was another Ray Smith also on Island Records – a member of Heads Hands & Feet – and as both had been inadvertently allocated each other's royalties on occasion, ex-Hackensack

Ray changed his name to Ray Major. Answering an advertisement in *Melody Maker* for a guitarist to join a 'name band', he rang up to ask who it was. The answer was that he couldn't be told yet, but if he came to the studio at a particular date and time, he would be auditioned. On arrival, he was welcomed by Overend, who immediately said he knew and liked Ray, was confident he would fit in and wanted him in the band. The brief audition was no more than a formality. They had previously considered John Cann of Atomic Rooster, Dave Ball of Procol Harum, Zal Cleminson from The Sensational Alex Harvey Band, and John Miles (later of 'Music' fame), but with his Mott connections, Ray was clearly the one.

Finding a new singer was more problematic, and at one stage, Overend was poised to take the job himself in addition to playing bass. They'd known all along that seeking somebody similar to Ian would not work; as Morgan said, 'There aren't any anyway!'. CBS suggested Russ Ballard, who'd left Argent the previous year, but Dale stressed that they'd prefer someone who didn't wear dark glasses like Ian, was younger than them, had a wide vocal range and was still relatively unknown. These factors might've counted against Russ, but his proven track record as a songwriter, singer and multi-instrumentalist might've made him the right choice after all. A Ballard-Watts songwriting partnership alone, if given the chance, would've been hard to beat. Interestingly, nobody contacted Russ on the subject, and he remained unaware that CBS had even put his name forward until contacted forty-plus years later by the present author.

The group's other ideas for vocalists included Stevie Wright from The Easybeats, Graham Bonnet, Robert Palmer and Pete French from Beck, Bogart & Appice. John Otway was auditioned, but the group thought they might inhibit him. Overend, in particular, wanted Nils Lofgren – who, though American, 'was small, and thus easy to hit around', and, more seriously, was a good singer, and in Overend's estimation, the best guitar player in the world.

It would be a recommendation from the ever-supportive Mick Ralphs that came to their rescue. He'd seen the virtually-unknown Nigel Benjamin at the Marquee fronting a band called Royce. Although only twenty years old, Benjamin was proficient on guitar, piano and vocals, and had already been in several other bands: one of which – Grott – also included Lee Brilleaux until he left to help form Dr. Feelgood. At the audition, Benjamin came across very well, not least because he had a good range and could hit the high notes. And despite – if not because of – his youth, he seemed like ideal frontman material.

After a few days of rehearsal, Mott (with their newly-truncated name) began sessions at Clearwell Castle on 28 April, using Ronnie Lane's Mobile Studio, producing themselves. Overdubs and mixing were then done with Geoff Emerick at AIR London Studio 3 in Oxford Street between 23 May and 9 June. Fourteen tracks had been completed, and eleven were selected for the album. The songs were all group originals, with the majority written by Overend. They were also offered a demo of 'Milk Train' – written by Dominic Bugatti and Frank Musker – but chose to pass on it. Roger Daltrey covered the song later that year on his solo album *Ride A Rock Horse*.

In self-deprecating fashion, Overend admitted the songs were written largely out of 'desperation'. As the only group member with any proven writing experience (culminating in one track on *The Hoople*), he was the one best placed to contribute. It became clear to them all that Nigel was fine as a vocalist but was unlikely to be able to write anything suitable for them, so it fell to bassist Overend to fill the role. By his own admission, he was writing material that was 'half good' – admitting he was not a natural with choruses: so, many of his numbers simply lacked one. His approach was to come up with a riff and try to finish it. But without any real song at the end, many of them were just 'two-thirds of the way there'. Moreover, he seldom wrote about specific incidents as Ian had done, but 'more general and imaginary' subject matter.

In spite of that, recording the album was great fun for Overend. They'd shaken off the burden of Mott The Hoople, and were a band again – a more-democratic unit, minus the add-ons of female backing vocalists, saxes or a string section that Overend felt were so unnecessary.

Though Morgan's contributions were more a matter of arrangement than songcraft, he agreed that the new lineup presented new opportunities for them all. There had been no resentment of Ian as a gifted writer with his own track record, as his lyrics had something to say, although the others didn't pay too much attention to the words at the time, as they were concentrating on the instrumental side. However, now that they were writing for themselves, they looked for riffs and chords before lyrics and melody. It went without saying that Ian had been a better songwriter all round. But without him out front, this was a new band with a new – more of a musician's – approach.

That summer, they played a few shows in Europe. The setlist was built predominantly around material from the new album *Drive On*, along with 'Rock And Roll Queen', 'Violence', 'Sweet Jane', 'All The Young Dudes' and

The Easybeats' 'Good Times'. The album's first single 'Monte Carlo' hit the shops on 22 August, and the group performed it a few days later on an episode of *Disco*: a short-lived Sunday afternoon (hardly prime-time viewing exposure) BBC TV pop-quiz series hosted by Terry Wogan. The album appeared in the shops on 12 September: Nigel's 21st birthday.

Drive On (Mott) (1975)
Personnel:
Nigel Benjamin: vocals
Ray Major: lead guitar, vocals
Overend Watts.: bass, vocals
Morgan Fisher: piano, organ, synthesiser, vocals
Dale Griffin: drums, vocals
Producer: Mott
Studio: Ronnie Lane's Mobile Studio at Clearwell Castle; AIR, London, April-June 1975
Release date: 12 September 1975
Chart placings: UK: 45, US: 160
Running time: 42:00
All songs written by Overend Watts unless stated otherwise.
Side One: 1. By Tonight 2. Monte Carlo 3. She Does It 4. I'll Tell You Something 5. Stiff Upper Lip
Side Two: 1. Love Now 2. Apologies (Major) 3. The Great White Wail 4. Here We Are 5. It Takes One To Know One (Griffin) 6. I Can Show You How It Is (Watts / Griffin)
Bonus track on 2014 reissue:
12. Shout It All Out

In retrospect, reviewers at the time and ever since have been divided about the two post-Ian Hunter Mott albums. Some have dismissed them as musical garbage and a miserable effort to walk in their former leader's shadow. Others recognise the records as good, solid rock that might lack the Hunter lyrical gift, but still have a distinctive swagger and strong, memorable riffs if not instantly catchy choruses, with Nigel's remarkable vocal range marking him out as another Steve Marriott or a British version of Rush's Geddy Lee.

Slightly edited versions of three tracks – 'Monte Carlo' in August (damned by *NME* as 'irritatingly heavy bubblegum'), 'By Tonight' in October, and a rare Dale composition 'It Takes One To Know One' in February the following year – made their way onto 45s in Britain, the first two likewise in Germany, and 'Monte Carlo' in Portugal and New Zealand, but to very little radio interest and zero chart action. All of them thrive on good infectious hooks – 'Monte Carlo' being easily the star exhibit, with some startling synth washes and a suitably-stinging guitar solo to match. 'She Does It' is an energetic and frenzied if otherwise unexceptional rocker, and 'I'll Tell You Something' is a bold stab at a power ballad, some years before the term became common musical parlance. A less menacing sequel to 'Pearl 'n' Roy', 'Stiff Upper Lip' is a tongue-in-cheek song about people moaning over the state of Britain – 'People feeling down 'cos they ain't got a pound' – with a spoken Hooray-Henry-style interlude asking the mob what all the bickering is about. Despite some fine piano wizardry, it comes across as an amusing but rather half-baked effort at a comic number and lacking Ian's flair as a wordsmith.

On side two, 'Love Now' is a sturdy rocker, while 'The Great White Wail' comes across as halfway between slow, menacing hard rock à la Led Zeppelin or Deep Purple and 1990s grunge. The barely-one-minute-long interlude 'Apologies' – featuring Nigel on a solo vocal and acoustic guitar – is the germ of an idea crying out for development, while 'Here We Are' and 'I Can Show You How It Is' are both gentle ballads – the latter a short song with a veiled reference to Ian in the lyric: 'Always being insecure's the price you have to pay'.

From the end of October until early-January 1976, the group toured America, headlining on some dates, and supporting Kiss, Aerosmith, Styx and REO Speedwagon on others. Comprising around 40 dates, it was a longer tour than any they'd undertaken with the previous lineup, and they generally received favourable reviews. Cries of 'Where are Ian and Mick?' were very much in the minority. The album sold about 120,000 copies there and spent five weeks in the lower reaches of the *Billboard* 200 chart. In Britain, it clipped the top 50 for only one week.

Chapter Seven: 1976

By the beginning of 1976, Ian was writing another new album, recording demos and auditioning new musicians. This time, Chris Stainton – previously Joe Cocker's right-hand man during his initial success with The Grease Band, and subsequently a member of Spooky Tooth – became his musical director and arranger. Originally, Stainton's main instrument had been bass, but with Ian, he took over on keyboards. At first, Dennis Elliott returned to rehearsals on drums, then left to join the newly-formed Foreigner. Elliott was replaced by Aynsley Dunbar, who had worked with John Mayall's Bluesbreakers, The Jeff Beck Group, The Mothers, and had recently joined Journey. Jaco Pastorius, well known for his work with Weather Report, came in on bass. Saxophonist David Sanborn had played on recent albums by David Bowie and Stevie Wonder, and was recruited along with Gerry Weems: guitarist with Bonaroo, who'd supported Hunter-Ronson on tour the previous year.

Ian admitted that when they were planning the new album, he was petrified by the idea of producing, writing and arranging alongside people who were the best in their profession. He was the first to admit he never had the technical ability of such people, even though he had a strong track record as a successful songwriter and frontman.

The basic work took place at his home in January, then recording took a further three weeks at Electric Lady Studios in New York, with Ian and Chris doing a final week of mixing at A&M Studios in Los Angeles. Twelve songs were recorded, but four didn't make the final cut.

All American Alien Boy (Ian Hunter) (1976)
Personnel:
Ian Hunter: vocals, rhythm guitar, piano
Chris Stainton: piano, organ, Mellotron, bass
Jaco Pastorius: bass, guitar
Aynsley Dunbar: drums, percussion
Gerry Weems: lead guitar
David Sanborn: alto saxophone
Cornell Dupree: guitar
John Gustafson: bass
Don Alias: congas
Arnie Lawrence: clarinet
Dave Bargeron: trombone

Lewis Soloff: trumpet
Ann E. Sutton, Gail Kantor, Erin Dickens, Freddie Mercury, Brian May, Roger Taylor,
Bob Segarini: backing vocals
Producer: Ian Hunter
Studio: Electric Lady, New York City, January 1976
Release date: 21 May 1976
Chart placings: UK: 29, US: 177
Running time: 40:09
All songs by Ian Hunter
Side One: 1. Letter To Brittania From The Union Jack 2. All American Alien Boy
3. Irene Wilde 4. Restless Youth
Side Two: 1. Rape 6. You Nearly Did Me In 7. Apathy 83 8. God (Take 1)
Bonus tracks 2006.
9. To Rule Britannia From The Union Jack (Outtake) 10. All American Alien Boy
(Single version) 11. Irene Wilde (Number One) (Outtake) 12. Weary Anger (Outtake)
13. Apathy (Outtake) 14. (God) Advice To A Friend (Outtake)

All American Alien Boy was something of a concept album, much of
it inspired by Ian's move across the Atlantic, and based partly on ideas
and material he'd carried around for a long time. This was going to be a
change of direction, moving more towards jazz rock territory. The opening
track 'Letter To Brittania From The Union Jack' with its lullaby-like Fender
Rhodes and Mellotron, is a bittersweet farewell to his fatherland – critical
of what Britain had become, but tinged with regret and sympathy:

You been through many things
I know you been around
I have fought armies for you in the conflict of the past

The fadeout cuts suddenly to the title track – seven minutes (edited to
just under four for the single) of a punchy, jazz-like groove, over which he
sings about packing his bags, and of his political detachment:

Don't wanna vote for the left wing
Don't wanna vote for the right
I gotta have both, to make me fly

He remembers the good times up and down the M1, but change is
coming: 'Look out Lennon, here I come/Land ahoy ahoy'. Over a sturdy

framework of piano and lead guitar, saxophone lines curl around the lead and gospel backing vocals, and there's even a short bass solo.

'Irene Wilde' was written for a girl from his days as a sixteen-year-old. She was an unattainable beauty from 'a Barker Street bus station non-affair' who treated him with scorn and who inadvertently inspired him to 'Be a somebody someday'. 'Restless Youth' is the closest the album comes to hard rock, though it's relatively slow – again, grunge before its time, with plenty of mean, lean and vicious guitar, and lyrics tackling America's criminal underworld and the Mafia.

On side two, the slow but angry gospel-flavoured 'Rape' treads dangerous ground but writes about violation and abuse without glorifying them in any way. It's a chilling lyric concluding with the ending's shouted verdict: 'Justice is – Not!'. Ian had evidently not forgotten his Dylan-inspired musical roots.

In view of Ian's strong bond with Queen, it came as no surprise to find three-quarters of them providing backing vocals on the next track. Originally titled 'Weary Anger', 'You Nearly Did Me In' is a plaintive ballad with soulful sax over the piano intro. The song was thought to refer to Mick Ronson and the Tony DeFries issues but was actually a bleak, semi-resigned comment on the American drug situation – one of 'lonely shadows/Silver needles abandoned in the evening war'.

'Apathy 83' is Ian's dismissive comment on the slow decay of a once vibrant rock scene. Over predominant congas and accordion, he sings, 'There ain't no rock 'n' roll no more/Just the sickly sound of greed'. He explained that he used the term 'rock 'n' roll' as a substitute for innocence – for him, it was Little Richard and Fats Domino, not Soft Machine 'and a lot of apathetic bands'. The lyric's repeated phrase 'Apathy for the Devil' was not a reference to the Rolling Stones classic, so much as a succinct comment made by Bob Dylan, who Ian met for the first time after they both caught the group at a rather uninspired show at Madison Square Garden.

The concluding 'God (Take 1)' was Ian's most Dylan-sounding song for a while. Over rhythm guitar and Al Kooper-ish organ, he sings of conducting a dialogue with God about good and evil, faith and the state of the world. Ian plays his cards close to his chest, questioning religion but remaining strictly neutral on his own religious beliefs.

The album lyrics are included on an insert sheet, and the inner bag includes a colour drawing of Ian without his shades.

Critics were understanding of the very different Ian Hunter on this album, praising him for what were his most adventurous, powerful and thoughtful songs to date. *All American Alien Boy* became a top 30 album in Britain but did considerably less well in America. Edited versions of the title track and 'You Nearly Did Me In' both failed completely as singles, despite the latter featuring three of Queen, who were riding the crest of a wave in Britain at the time.

Having been so enthusiastic about the album on its completion, Ian had second thoughts, later dubbing it commercial suicide. Though first-class musicians were playing on it, he thought it 'was all slow and pretty boring, but it was something I just wanted to do'. He didn't tour to promote it, and 1976 would be the first year for a long time that he didn't play a single gig. Columbia Records in America remained ever-supportive but began to wonder whether Ian's future with them lay in a non-performing capacity, such as in international A&R. When he asked what duties this would entail, he was told it would mean things like meeting Ray Conniff off his plane. It didn't take Ian long to say no.

The new Mott had mixed fortunes with their first album, but it looked like a solid base to build on. In February 1976, they went into The Manor studio to begin work on a second album. The provisional title *The Side of a Wedding in Germany* – a bizarre idea that Pete thought up – was discarded in favour of *Shouting and Pointing* – taken from an Oliver Reed interview where he said that was the way he used to discipline his sons. After having planned the first album carefully before entering the studio, this time, they decided to keep it more spontaneous, aiming for a tougher, more experimental set. A second American tour was planned but postponed slightly when the sessions took longer than planned.

CBS made a token effort to keep the old group name alive when they released *Greatest Hits* in March. The twelve tracks comprised three album tracks and all their A-sides from 'All The Young Dudes' onwards, with 'Saturday Gig' now renamed 'The Saturday Gigs'. When the record made no chart impression, it was a sad indication of how quickly they'd slipped from the public eye, even though the last two singles (admittedly the least successful) were making their first appearance on an album. Charles Shaar Murray's *NME* review took issue with the track selection, observing that Mick Ronson was merely mentioned as guitarist on the last track, was accorded no mention in the liner notes, or given a single picture, and inferred that some pettiness on behalf of the band's new incarnation was a major factor in not giving 'the dude his due'.

The group co-produced *Shouting and Pointing* with Eddie Kramer, who'd previously worked with the likes of Jimi Hendrix and Kiss. Everything went smoothly enough until Pete, Dale and Eddie flew to New York to mix the album. There they discovered sound quality problems – only resolved when they took the tapes back to England, where old friend Bill Price from the Mott The Hoople days helped them complete the job at Wessex Studios in Highbury.

They then rehearsed for a short British tour to coincide with the album's 4 June release, but three dates were cancelled when Ray Major was prevented from playing because of a cyst on his hand. He recovered in time for the remaining three – the final being at Victoria Palace on 13 June. Later that month, they played 'Shouting and Pointing' live on Manchester's Granada TV show *So It Goes*. Presenter Tony Wilson introduced them as a band who'd just shortened their name, 'now that Mick Ralphs is playing with unsavoury company, and now that Ian Hunter's playing with himself – we can say that now he's a tax exile'.

Shouting And Pointing (Mott) (1976)

Personnel:
Nigel Benjamin: vocals
Ray Major: lead guitar, vocals
Overend Watts: bass, vocals
Morgan Fisher: piano, organ, synthesizer, vocals
Dale Griffin: drums, vocals
Additional personnel:
Mick Ralphs: bass
Stan Tippins: backing vocals
Producers: Mott and Eddie Kramer
Studio: The Manor, Shipton on Cherwell, February-March 1976
Release date: 4 June 1976
Chart placings: UK: -, US: -
Running time: 42:00
Side One: 1. Shouting and Pointing (Watts / Fisher) 2. Collision Course (Watts) 3. Storm (Watts / Fisher / Major) 4. Career (No Such Thing As Rock 'n' Roll) (Fisher / Benjamin)
Side Two: 1. Hold On, You're Crazy (Watts) 2. See You Again (Watts) 3. Too Short Arms (I Don't Care) (Watts / Major) 4. Broadside Outcasts (Watts / Fisher) 5. Good Times (Harry Vanda / George Young)

Bonus track 2014

10. Too Short Arms (I Don't Care) (Watts / Major) (Eddie Kramer/Electric Lady Mix)

Like the previous album, *Shouting And Pointing* got a mixed reception – at the time, and again on its re-release decades later. While some had still not forgiven the band for continuing without Ian, others were more open-minded, judging the band on their own merits. Although Overend admitted that an additional experienced songwriter would surely have been to his benefit – adding something to his riffs – the band still packed a mighty punch. Morgan's keyboard playing – which sometimes sounded like barrelhouse piano but far superior – was always a highlight and can be heard to great effect on the title track, which he co-wrote.

'Collision Course' is one moment where they hit on a strong chorus, enhanced by vocal harmonies that recall Sweet at their best. There's also a killer slide guitar, and lyrics like 'Don't let them tell you you'll never find fame/We know better!' – and after the final chord, a swift 'Hello, boys' from Overend's parrot Toby.

'Storm' has a driving guitar and piano sound, but also a welcome burst of light and shade with delicate piano and synths, building with the aid of a few bombastic guitar chords, not unlike Kansas or the coming Toto in their more rock-meets-classical moments.

Nigel's sole songwriting contribution (in collaboration with Morgan) is 'Career (No Such Thing As Rock 'n' Roll)' – the album's only ballad and an ambitious, confessional song that suggests a desire to walk in Ian's shoes with a more introspective piece about the music business. Morgan noted that Nigel was good on ballads, saying this track turned out 'spectacularly well', and it was the peak of their work together in Mott.

Side two begins with Overend handling vocals on 'Hold On, You're Crazy' It's a song with another great hook, and forceful guitar and synths – the sheer wall of sound though compensating for a song that never quite gets there.

'See You Again' is a more tender, slow number, with acoustic and slide guitars, and attractive vocal harmonies. 'Too Short Arms (I Don't Care)' is undoubtedly the best track of all: a lighthearted song of waking up late the morning after the night before. A glorious burst of Morgan's barrelhouse piano wizardry produces what is perhaps the most infectious instrumental break any line-up of Mott ever recorded. Had the CBS executives been doing their job properly, the song's single potential would've been staring them in the face. A remastered version of the album released on CD in 2009 included as a bonus track an 'Eddie Kramer/ Electric Lady mix', about fifteen seconds longer, without the few seconds of studio chat at the start, and guitar more prominent in the mix.

'Broadside Outcasts' with its stately guitar and piano intro, sounds like another ambitious effort about the state of the country in 1976, and its refrain of 'There's an earthquake coming/Gonna knock you all flat/ What you gonna do about that?' Surely the measured tones of then-Prime Minister James Callaghan on the fade-out raised a smile from some: 'The government's aim, repeat, drive on'.

The old Easybeats' favourite 'Good Times' that always went down well live, rounds the record off in style. Mott had also considered recording The Doors' 'Love Me Two Times' – which they often played in concert, interpolating drums and bass parts from The Sorrows' 'Take A Heart' – but they decided against it, thinking one cover version to be enough for one album.

The front and back sleeve photos – the end result of around two weeks of planning – were designed to represent a rock and roll battlefield. Morgan was attired as a shouty-looking military officer in smart uniform and peaked cap, surrounded by his longer-haired colleagues amidst assorted musical equipment and paraphernalia, with a glowing sunset behind them.

An *NME* review concluded, 'I bet they're amazing live'. The gigs were packed. They always attracted favourable live reviews, and if anything, they generally sounded tighter on stage than the old band had – if a couple of CDs of live British and American gigs released many years later is anything to go by.

Shouting and Pointing was released simultaneously on both sides of the Atlantic and elsewhere but failed to chart. Having lifted three unsuccessful singles off the first album, CBS didn't even release *one* this time round, and the album died a death.

A few live dates in America followed in July, on the same bill as Rush and Blue Oyster Cult. In Dale's view, the tour was the usual half-hearted effort on the part of management. He drew up a constructive, detailed plan on how he felt they needed to work and be promoted properly there, but found the managerial team to be totally unreceptive. For all the problems that constantly beset Mott – most of them of a financial nature – the group's reception in the States was very positive, but the management and record company could barely be bothered to take any notice, let alone deal with it head-on. Their American manager Fred Heller told Dale that if he didn't like the way he was managing the group, he could go back to pumping gas. They saw this as a good example of the contempt in which Heller held 'dumb rock musicians'. They'd already split from their British manager Bob Hirschman and had set up a new management office of their own in Acton, run by Gerry Mantell-Sayer, who'd been part of Hirschman's team with Stan Tippins and Chris Whitehouse.

Another personnel issue made matters worse. Prior to what would be the final British tour, four of them realised that Nigel was not the vocalist they wanted. Dale decided he wasn't singing from the same hymn sheet as the rest. Morgan thought there was 'just too much mucking about', and he and Nigel nearly came to blows once. It gradually dawned on them that they missed Ian's powerful presence centre-stage, the keyboard player opined: 'Having a multi-octave voice doth not a frontman maketh.'

Overend thought Nigel had problems with improvising – which was clearly at odds with their love of spontaneity and keeping things a little loose – and saw himself as a Peter Gabriel-type figure. Moreover, he was several years younger than the rest and there was something of a generation-gap problem in that they never had any jam sessions with him because he was too young to know the old standard rock'n'roll numbers they had been familiar with while growing up. A Velvet Revolution would be the answer, with Morgan, Overend and Dale having a secret meeting with Kelvin Blacklock: a long-time fan who played them some demos featuring himself as vocalist. They held some rehearsals with him, and at first, were sufficiently impressed to consider asking him to join, then giving Nigel the sack. But they had second thoughts when it became apparent that Kelvin didn't measure up, so Nigel stayed where he was.

It was a matter of some concern to CBS that Mott's chart success had been almost negligible over the last two years, and their contract was up for renewal. Early in September, they went to Pye Studios at Marble Arch for what would be a final recording session. Overend had written a new number initially called 'Cross That Line', which then became 'Get Rich Quick'. Nicky Graham, a CBS A&R executive, excitedly told them that it was 'top-10 material', maybe even top-3. Sadly, they were unable to contact him for the next few days. By then, CBS had passed on their option to extend their contract.

Though they were now without a record label, on 16 October, Mott recorded a BBC Radio 1 *In Concert*, including 'Get Rich Quick' and Little Richard's 'I Don't Wanna Discuss It', and much of the next few weeks were taken up by a tour of Britain including several university and polytechnic gigs.

By the time of the final dates in mid-November, it was also the end of the road for Mott. Morgan admitted that without Ian, they never had much of a chance, with none of them being natural songwriters, and trying to force new singers into a Hunter-shaped hole didn't work. Nigel never felt very comfortable in the role, and they never gave him the chance to do what he wanted anyway. When they did give him some chances, they rejected what he came up with, 'because we really couldn't get into what he was doing'. 'Career (No Such Thing As Rock 'n' Roll)' was the exception. Nigel was frustrated, as they felt his songs were unsuitable for Mott, and the friction escalated until it was longer tenable. Later, he recalled one of the last things Overend said to him when they were on the road: 'Nigel, I know you're upset, we'd like to do more of your material. But you don't understand, this is my last chance'. The others respected that Overend was the only member with any real claim to being a songwriter. Nigel concluded bitterly that they weren't playing music because it was good, but because it was their bassist's last opportunity to make a few bucks. About an hour later, Nigel started planning out his future and picked up the phone. On a later occasion, he met Ian in a pub across the street from the Hammersmith Odeon, and they talked, after which Nigel realised he'd left the band for the same reasons Ian had two years earlier.

Coincidentally, at the end of the year, there were rumours that Ian was being invited to join Uriah Heep or The Doors, or even a reformed Mott The Hoople. There was some truth in the first two. He said the comparative failure of *All American Alien Boy* had effectively killed his career. David Byron had been sacked from Uriah Heep after heavy drinking made him unreliable. Ian was offered a sizeable fee to replace him, and was given copies of their albums with specific tracks marked that they would want him to sing, but he said he didn't really like the band's music. As for The Doors, Ian said succinctly that he was a lyricist but no oil-painting like Jim Morrison.

Where Ian's old group was concerned, he said the stupidity in the ranks had often driven him to despair, and he felt really sad about where they were now: 'I worked for that name for years, and I hate to see it slowly go down'. The only way forward was to put a new band of his own together.

Chapter Eight: 1977

Having to a large extent reinvented himself as a born-again but not very successful jazz rocker, and left rock and roll behind, Ian reverted to type. Over the last few months of 1976, what had become a rather stagnant music scene on both sides of the Atlantic was finding a new energy in punk. In New York, The Ramones and Patti Smith spearheaded the list of new acts to watch. Ian went to see several bands there, was impressed with the stirrings of something new, and it rekindled his enthusiasm.

Returning to London, he recruited several British and American musicians, including Peter Oxendale – former keyboard player with The Glitter Band and Jet – and bassist Bob Rawlinson who'd worked with Stan Webb of Chicken Shack. Through Mick Ronson, Ian met guitarist Earl Slick, who'd been in a band with Roy Bittan and would become a Bruce Springsteen sideman. Dennis Elliott was Ian's first choice as drummer, but Elliott was in the process of forming Foreigner. A replacement was found in Mac Poole, who'd been in Broken Glass with Peter Oxendale and Ian's old friend Miller Anderson. By December, they were rehearsing new songs at Milner Sound Studios in Chelsea – Ian having decided that the album was to be called *Overnight Angels*: as was the band.

Early in the new year, they went to a studio at Morin Heights, Quebec, with Roy Thomas Baker: best known for producing Queen. But Ian and the band were dissatisfied with Mac Poole's work, so Denis Elliott was contacted and came to complete it. Everything was brought to a halt on the night of 3 February when the house they were staying in was destroyed by fire. They all escaped, but four of them were briefly admitted to hospital, and Roy had injured his hand. All their personal possessions were lost, among them Earl's treasured guitar.

Sessions resumed a few days later, and in March, Ian went to London to record extra vocals at Utopia and Olympic Studios. Mixing was completed at Sarm Studios, and the record was mastered at Sterling Sound, New York. '(Miss) Silver Dime' had been chosen as a single but was replaced with 'Justice Of The Peace': released on 13 May, with the album following a week later.

Ian Hunter's Overnight Angels (Ian Hunter) (1977)
Personnel:
Ian Hunter: vocals, rhythm guitar, piano
Earl Slick: lead, rhythm and slide guitars

Peter Oxendale: keyboards
Rob Rawlinson: bass, harmony vocals
Dennis Elliott: drums
Miller Anderson, Lem Lubin: harmony vocals
Roy Thomas Baker: percussion
Producer: Roy Thomas Baker
Studios: Le Studio, Morin Heights, Quebec; Utopia Studios, Primrose Hill, London; Olympic Studios, London, January-March 1977
Release date: 20 May 1977
Chart placings: UK: -, US: unreleased
Running time: 37:33
All songs by Ian Hunter unless otherwise stated.
Side One: 1. Golden Opportunity 2. Shallow Crystals 3. Overnight Angels
4. Broadway
Side Two: 1. Justice Of The Peace 2. (Miss) Silver Dime (Hunter / Earl Slick)
3. Wild N' Free 4. Ballad Of Little Star 5. To Love A Woman
Bonus track
10. England Rocks

Those who thought *All American Alien Boy* was a little too far from Ian's usual style were reassured by his full-blooded return to base. 'Golden Opportunity' made a strong opening track, beginning with 90 seconds of keyboard instrumental with a subtle tempo change and prominent bass runs, before Ian kicked into a song inspired by his disenchantment with British politicians who had reduced the country to such a state:

The kids are OK
They're telling you now
But you're letting them down
Cause you just don't know how

'Shallow Crystals' – originally titled 'I Think You Made A Mess Of His Life' – was thought to have been directed at either David Bowie, Guy Stevens or Verden Allen. Ian remained non-committal, saying it may have been 'a selection of ideas and words that were attracted to each other'. A plaintive ballad, it provides a good setting for Earl's striking guitar solo.

'Overnight Angels' is an atmospheric song with interesting whooshing instrumental effects to match the slightly surreal lyrics: angels 'Dancing through the toys of the dead and the living/Laughing at the poets changing their rhymes'. Ian was later dismissive of it, saying he liked the sound of the title, but otherwise, it was 'a plastic attempt to get (rock 'n' roll) back on the record'. To close side one, 'Broadway' is an appealing ballad – a commentary on the ups and downs of showbusiness and the dreams of aspiring would-be stars.

The single 'Justice Of The Peace' is easily the most commercial track – a song about a shotgun wedding, introduced by a few seconds of Mendelssohn's *Wedding March*, and featuring a frantic vocal. *Sounds* praised it and wrongly predicted a hit – lack of airplay killing its chances.

'(Miss) Silver Dime' – the other possible single – is an epic ballad, a slow, dreamy tune that builds up to a huge chorus. The frantic 'Wild 'N Free' rings the changes again. 'Ballad Of Little Star' – intended for the previous album but shelved – is a lament for the plight of the modern native-American in an unsympathetic nation, much of it backed by sparse and tender piano. Finally, 'To Love A Woman' is probably the least interesting song, oddly middle-of-the-road by Ian's usual standards and sounding like a half-hearted attempt at disco, but without the energy.

The album was released in a gatefold sleeve, the front cover and inner sections featuring two Ian portraits. The cover was a black and white side view of his face, his hair a mass of metal coils and feathers; the inner, by artist David Oxtoby, showed half his face and skull surrounded by two huge dark blue wings with a mountain of flames in the background.

Most of the press reaction was favourable, *Sounds* calling it 'a barrage of rock'n'roll napalm', while to *Record Mirror* it was 'pure dynamite', adding that 'The guv'nor's back doing what comes naturally – rocking hard'. *NME*, on the other hand, headlined its unenthusiastic review with 'Overweight Angels'.

According to Roy Thomas Baker, Ian was initially very pleased with the album. Later, he more or less disowned it, saying that on much of it, he was forced to pitch his voice artificially high, saying it was 'a mistake', the worst album he'd ever done, and the only one he really regretted making.

Ian's Overnight Angels played several dates in England in the first two weeks of June. Dennis was unable to take part – his place at the drums taken by Curly Smith: former member of Jo Jo Gunne. The setlist included several tracks from the album alongside 'Once Bitten Twice Shy', One Of The Boys', 'Roll Away The Stone', 'All The Way From Memphis' and, inevitably, 'All The Young Dudes'. The encores were comprised of 'Cleveland Rocks': a song he'd just written and recorded and tactfully reworked as 'England Rocks', and 'Whole Lotta Shakin' Goin' On'.

A few days earlier, Ian caused mild controversy in an interview when he said they'd be supporting ELO at Earl's Court, adding that they were 'completely boring and we'll kill them'. Instead, they headlined at the Hammersmith Odeon, where he met ELO's manager Don Arden and explained he'd been joking, as he had the greatest respect for the band. Ian was about to be temporarily without a record deal, and at one point, it seemed as if Arden might be trying to sign Ian to the Jet label.

As they played 'England Rocks' at the Hammersmith Odeon, an avalanche of paper union jacks with 'England Rocks' printed across them dropped from the ceiling onto the audience, in line with Britain that week celebrating the Queen's silver jubilee. Whatever his views (or lack of them) on the celebrations may have been, Ian didn't look back on the English dates with any great affection. Afterwards, he said he was writing, playing and singing really badly, 'and I hated the whole mess I was in'.

After it became obvious that the minimal airplay given to 'Justice Of The Peace' was not going to make it a hit, 'England Rocks' was issued as a stand-alone single on 22 July, to good reviews. But if CBS had hoped to capitalise on jubilee fever, their hopes were dashed. Rainbow bassist Jimmy Bain sang backing vocals on the record and was offered a place in Overnight Angels, but his replacement in Rainbow left after a few weeks, and Bain returned to the fold.

But not even live appearances could make 'England Rocks' a hit in Britain, and partly due to issues resulting from Ian severing his association with manager Fred Heller, Columbia did not issue the single or album in America. The title doubtless also had some bearing on the matter.

In the intervening years, some rock critics have damned *Overnight Angels* as a poor album. But at least one fan was a passionate admirer. During the Overnight Angels tour, aspiring seventeen-year-old rock singer Joe Elliott and a friend made their way towards the Mott dressing room and Ian invited them in. Forming Def Leppard a year or two later, Joe became one of the most fervent champions of Ian Hunter and Mott The Hoople, and would cover several of their songs.

While in England, Ian went to see some of the punk shows. Some had regarded Mott The Hoople as being punks before their time. But Ian was unimpressed with much of what he saw and heard, remarking that the term 'new wave' seemed specifically aimed at rejecting people like him as 'old wave'. He pointed out that ageism was just as bad as racism. When DJ Jeff Dexter took Ian to see The Damned at The Roxy, Ian asked, 'Was that what we were like?' "Yeah", replied Jeff, "but *you* were great". However, it soon emerged that The Clash considered Ian to be a major influence.

Shortly after Mott disbanded, singer-songwriter Steve Hyams came to visit Overend. Around the time Mott The Hoople recorded their first album in 1969, Overend bumped into Steve, who was then working on the record counter at the Chelsea Drugstore – a record shop much loved by young wannabe musicians, and namechecked in The Rolling Stones' 'You Can't Always Get What You Want'. Steve rented a room for a while in the band's flat in Lower Sloane Street. He sang and played guitar with a couple of bands, signed a contract as a solo artist with Phonogram and recorded an album which was pressed but then withdrawn, all copies destroyed. Towards the end of 1974, Overend, Dale and Morgan helped him out on a session. A couple of years later, after Nigel Benjamin had left Mott, contact with Steve was renewed. They had a few rehearsals at Overend's home and then – between January and March 1977 – recorded some demos at The Argonaut: Richard Branson's floating barge studio on Regent's Park Canal. Apart from 'International Heroes', by Kim Fowley and Kerry Scott, Steve wrote all of the songs, some complemented with additional sections from Overend. But Dale was unhappy with the thin, harsh and distorted sound. He believed there was a problem with the Argonaut mixing desk.

Meanwhile, Steve tried to persuade them to resurrect the name Mott The Hoople, but they were undecided, and Steve thought they still hoped Ian would eventually return, particularly if his solo career looked like stalling after a promising start. Steve introduced them to a couple of businessmen he knew who could be potential managers, as long as he was the frontman. Though Dale was wary of an incoming vocalist trying to set himself up as leader in this way, he heard potential in the songs, but mainly because Overend had a hand in writing them. They were still keen to keep the band together in some way if possible, so meetings and discussions were held. They wanted to drop the name Mott, which now had increasingly negative connotations. The would-be managers, therefore, suggested they become Mott The Hoople again. It hardly mattered that they were playing very different music with different personnel, as Fleetwood Mac similarly reinvented themselves over the years, altering their style and becoming very successful in America. It was a persuasive proposition, but with the best will in the world, nobody could suggest that Steve – for all his promise as a songwriter – had anything like the stage presence or charisma of Lindsey Buckingham or Stevie Nicks.

Despite the others' reservations, Steve took the initiative, organising a concert showcase and photo session at the Rainbow Theatre for *Sounds* journalists. Dale was the one most opposed to the idea. For him, the Fleetwood Mac analogy would never work, especially in view of what he called Steve's introverted, shambling stage demeanour. When the performance started, Dale's worst fears were realised. Thinking the show itself was awful, at the end, he left the stage as soon as he could and initially refused to take part in the photo shoot. He was only persuaded to join in – against his better judgment – because he'd worked with and liked the shoot photographer Kate Simon, but he did his best to hide behind Morgan when the time came. In retrospect, it was – and always remained – one of the low points, if not the lowest, in his career.

Even Steve admitted that the recordings could've been better. He had faith in Dale and Overend's experience and ability to get the best out of a studio, and wished they'd been able to find a better one. Nevertheless, he was convinced they all felt positive about their work at the time and was confident the songs were good and were geared towards the new wave. Hirschman and Heller heard the tapes but were unsure whether there was a market for them. At this time, it was as if the only thing that really mattered to record companies in Britain was punk. The remains of an early-1970s band who'd seemingly gone out of fashion in a fickle business, were dropped by their last label and were plainly struggling to re-establish themselves with one new member after another would have an uphill battle.

Steve then took the tapes to Arista, who rejected them. Later that night, Arista phoned Steve at home, telling him they really liked the material and wanted to sign him as a solo artist, but that Mott had had their day. Ray conceded that Steve had written what he called 'good songs', and felt sorry for him over the divided loyalties situation. Although unhappy about letting his mates down, Steve accepted the invitation – partly in light of what he called his 'healthy drug habit', that an advance would surely help to fund – and began recording for Arista. A little later, Arista recruited new management, who promptly dropped twelve of their acts, including Steve.

The six demos sat on the shelf until 1993 when See For Miles Records released them on the mini-album *World Cruise,* which was named after the final track – credited to Mott The Hoople featuring Steve Hyams. After being deleted, Eastworld Recordings reissued it eight years later. When advised of the album's imminent appearance, Overend (the credited producer) and Dale both attempted to block it. The latter made it plain that the record was not by Mott The Hoople and was no more than a ragbag of hurried demos by Steve Hyams accompanied by Mott. It had never been intended for commercial release, 'and should not have been inflicted upon the public'. Dale would've been prepared to accept it as 'Mott with Steve Hyams', but in his view, anything else was downright misleading. The artwork bore a genuine-looking Mott The Hoople logo, and Overend had been denied songwriting credits on all but one of his collaborations..

World Cruise (Mott The Hoople featuring Steve Hyams)(1993)

Personnel:
Steve Hyams: vocals
Ray Major: lead guitar, vocals
Overend Watts: bass, vocals
Morgan Fisher: piano, organ, synthesizer, vocals
Dale Griffin: drums, vocals
Producer: Overend Watts
Studio: The Argonaut, near Maida Vale, London, January-March 1977
Release date: 1993 (See For Miles), 2001 (Eastworld)
Chart placings: UK: -, US: –
Running time: 21:09
All songs written by Steve Hyams unless stated otherwise.
Track listing: 1. Dear Louise 2. Brother Soul 3. Hotfootin' (Hyams / Watts) 4. Wild In The Streets (Garland Jeffreys) 5. 1.2.3.4. (Kickalong Blues) 6. World Cruise

The Mott The Hoople album that never was – or in their opinion never should've been – is really one for the completist. Steve Hyams had potential as a singer, but the songs are rather less than interesting. The playing is fair, but the group were basically doing a friend a favour. Listening to these six tracks is an oddly impersonal experience as if to suggest they were all merely going through the motions. Hearing the material cold, without knowing the background history, might've made it easier to judge on its own merits, but it lacks sparkle. The two much-maligned Mott albums that preceded it would rate at least three stars out of five with any fair-minded listener, but this deserves two at most. One cannot but sympathise wholeheartedly with Dale's blunt opinion. Perhaps the last word should be left for Steve's main friend in the band: Overend. He said Steve had a very unusual voice and great ability but was indecisive, and a lifelong drug habit was his undoing. Steve admitted that at the time the tracks were recorded, he had hepatitis, was on heroin, and was clearly not in a position to give of his best.

Morgan never lacked session work, but the others had ever-rising debts with no money coming in. For lack of any alternative, the search began again for a new singer. John Otway came close to filling the vacancy, but they thought he wouldn't be quite right. It was Morgan who provided the answer. Among those he'd worked with recently was John Fiddler of the recently disbanded Medicine Head. When Morgan suggested John as the obvious choice as a perfect frontman, Overend was unsure. To him, John seemed 'a bit hippy-ish and a little overweight', but Overend conceded he was a good writer with a good voice, and above all, had a worthwhile track record. One evening, John invited Morgan over for dinner, and the telephone kept ringing. Each time it was Overend asking Morgan, 'Have you asked him yet?'

John loved the idea, but having been in the music business for some years himself (being 30, he was seven years older than Nigel), he stipulated he would not be just another frontman for another incarnation of Mott. The group would play some of his songs, and it had to be a new band: all conditions to which they readily agreed.

All five musicians had a couple of rehearsals, and the chemistry was right immediately. John unveiled one of his latest songs, 'One More Chance To Run' – a pertinent title for them if ever there was one – and they all loved it. At another session in Kings Road, a man walked in carrying a guitar case. Overend didn't recognise him at first. It was John, with shorter, restyled hair, no moustache, no glasses, and looking about two stone thinner, like a resurrected Marc Bolan. Needing a new name, they toyed with the ideas of Mott The Savage, Mott The King or Mott The Lion, to attempt some continuity with their old moniker. When they took into account that it would be a completely new group and any links with their past would be inappropriate, they considered The Dambusters, Brain Haulage, Big Ben, Electric Fires, Landslide London and Gretna Brown. In the end, they chose British Lions. John didn't like it, but he conceded that their chances were likely to be slim at home, and the name would stand a good chance of helping them crack the American market.

Overend was particularly glad to be relieved of the burden of being the main songwriter, and it soon became clear he could add something to some of John's songs – John having already proven himself as a hit writer with four top-30 singles (one of them top-3) to his name within the last six years.

After completing some demos, they sought suitable management. A meeting with Chas Chandler – who'd successively guided Jimi Hendrix and Slade to stardom – proved unproductive, so they approached Status Quo's manager Colin Johnson. He was very enthusiastic, loved their songs and accordingly signed them to Phonogram – on the Vertigo label in Britain and RSO in America – and booked sessions at The Manor studio. Everything went off without a hitch. They originally went there with the intention of self-producing the A- and B-sides of two singles, with assistance from Mick Glossop, who'd been Eddie Kramer's tape operator on the *Shouting and Pointing* album. After four days, they'd completed not only these but the backing tracks for an entire album, so they decided to stay and finish the work.

Across November and December, they played 20 dates in Britain, several supporting Status Quo on their winter tour. After their debut at Sheffield Top Rank on 4 November, their manager Colin Johnson commented that by the time they started their third number, they were sending shivers down his spine. They were really working to be a part of what was going on in the audience, and the crowds loved them. Most of the set was built around the recorded album tracks, along with their own versions of 'Come On' and 'Wild One'.

Ray always remembered with amusement what happened after a gig when they supported Status Quo at the Apollo, Glasgow. He and Overend were in the hotel bar when they spotted The Shadows' Hank Marvin – the inspiration for a whole generation of young British guitarists – sitting quietly in a corner on his own sipping his fruit juice. Slightly drunk, Overend walked over and told Hank how he'd started him off playing guitar, and that when he was much younger, he even had a pair of sunglasses with the lenses removed so he could look like him and Buddy Holly. Soon, Overend was speaking to Hank more and more like an old mate, pointing out some mistakes he'd made on old Shadows records and naming specific tracks. Hank politely pointed out how, at the time, they didn't have the overdubbing facilities that were now available, so they had to keep going for a single take, and sometimes errors remained on the finished recordings. Still somewhat starstruck, Overend shook Hank's hand firmly, telling him how great it was to meet him. Hank then said he had to be off to Newcastle the next morning and quickly left.

For their final show of the year on 23 December, they played a Christmas party at Friar's Club, Aylesbury, with a set comprising much of their album and 'Rising Sun': a Medicine Head hit from 1973. Much to the delight of band and audience, Ian joined them on stage for an encore of 'All The Young Dudes': sadly not recorded. Even so, it gave British Lions quite a lift throughout the whole gig, knowing what was coming at the end. They could have also regarded his appearance as the ultimate Hunter seal of approval, one that the Nigel Benjamin-fronted Mott would never have received.

Chapter Nine: 1978

1978 would be an exceptionally quiet year for Ian Hunter, with no new releases to his name. He was temporarily without a manager, band or label. As if to compensate, he was suddenly much in demand to collaborate with and produce other artists. Through his friendship with Tuff Darts guitarist Jeff Salen, he played piano on two tracks on their eponymous album. They were one of the first punk bands to establish themselves at club CBGB in New York, but they never had any chart success and disbanded shortly afterwards.

After being contacted by Mott's former manager Robert Hirschman, Ian worked with Mr Big: the British band who had a top-5 hit with 'Romeo' the previous year. Their vocalist and main songwriter Dicken (Jeff Pain) was always a huge Mott The Hoople fan, and was keen to secure Ian's services for the third Mr Big album. Ian went to Chipping Norton Studios, Oxfordshire, to produce the sessions and play guitar, and along with Peter Oxendale, keyboards. They released the single 'Senora' in 1978, but the resulting album *Seppuku* was a hard-rocking collection, and not the pop confection EMI were expecting. They refused to release the album, and it eventually appeared on the Angel Air label in 2001.

A similar fate awaited another project Ian took part in that year when he joined Corky Laing of Mountain to help with demos for a second solo album. Among other musicians taking part were keyboard player Lee Michaels, former Free bassist Andy Fraser and former Alice Cooper guitarist Steve Hunter. For various personal or musical reasons, they didn't manage to work together, but it transpired that Mick Ronson was in the area, and – more importantly – was available. Ian had always regretted how management problems had halted their working arrangement a couple of years earlier, and they were delighted to be together again. Todd Rundgren came on board to add Hammond organ and backing vocals, and John Sebastian played harmonica. The only track written solely by Ian was 'The Outsider' (which would reappear in a different form on his forthcoming solo album). Credited to Laing, Hunter, Ronson and Pappalardi, *The Secret Sessions* was eventually released on Pet Rock Records in 1999, supplemented with a couple of bonus tracks, one featuring contributions from Eric Clapton and Dickey Betts.

Another super-session took place in New York shortly afterwards when Corky and Ian learned that John Cale was recording in an adjacent studio and Mick suggested they should invite him to join.

At the beginning of June, all four spontaneously decided to record an album and taped about an hour's worth of material. Ian always remembered the results fondly, remarking that all the lyrics were 'stream of consciousness', and that it was one of the few occasions on which he could reel off the lyrics without writing them down first. The participants were keen for 'the workshop tapes' to be released, but they've remained somewhere in the vaults ever since.

Having gotten over his creative disenchantment after what were (to him) the comparative failures of his last two solo albums, Ian started writing again. More importantly, being set free from CBS/Columbia, he was now able to work with Mick Ronson again and seek a new contract. Roy Eldridge – director of Chrysalis Records – contacted Ian, as Generation X bassist Tony James was very keen for him to produce their forthcoming album *Valley of the Dolls*. Roy had always been a Mott The Hoople fan, and as a past writer for *Melody Maker* and *Sounds*, had interviewed Ian before. Ian was interested, especially when he checked the papers and saw that Generation X were getting a good deal of press coverage. At the same time, he was interested in a new contract himself, and when he played some of his new demos for Roy, he was immediately impressed.

Ian said that working with Generation X was a mixed blessing, as the band knew what sound they were after, obviously loved rock and roll, and they all got on well. But producing them was hard work because they couldn't really play that well. The guitarist Derwood Andrews was fine, but Billy Idol's singing and Mark Laff's inadequate drumming posed a problem. To sort out the latter, Ian enlisted former Jethro Tull drummer Clive Bunker, and used both players together, getting a distinctive double-drum-kit sound. Recorded at Wessex Sound Studios, *Valley of the Dolls* was released in January 1979 and narrowly missed the top 50. But pressing the singles 'King Rocker' and 'Valley Of The Dolls' on several different colours of vinyl boosted sales, giving Generation X what would be their only top 30 hit.

To promote their forthcoming eponymous debut album, British Lions played a punishing schedule of gigs over the first few weeks of the new year – starting on 13 January at North Staffordshire Polytechnic, Stoke-on-Trent, and playing the Top Rank, Cardiff, the following evening. On 3 February, 'One More Chance To Run' took a bow as the first single, with the album following a week later. As Dale was at pains to make clear, it was a brand new band, and *not* Mott by another name. With their contemporary John Fiddler having a proven track record as singer, musician and writer, his joining the band energised everyone. Nevertheless, 1978 looked set to be a difficult year for those acts in Britain that were trying to get established but found themselves unwillingly lumped into the *old wave*. While the punk generation had not altered the 1977 music scene as effectively as the 1950s rock and roll pioneers had altered theirs, British Lions – effectively a brand new band – were nevertheless clearly going to find it a difficult market to compete in.

British Lions *(1978)*
Personnel:
John Fiddler: vocals, guitar
Ray Major: lead guitar, vocals
Morgan Fisher: keyboards, vocals
Overend Watts: bass, vocals
Dale Griffin: drums, vocals
Stan Tippins: backing vocals
Producer: British Lions
Studio: The Manor, September-October 1977
Release date: February 1978
Chart placings: UK: -, US: 83
Running time: 42:24
Side One: 1. One More Chance To Run (Fiddler) 2. Wild In The Streets (Garland Jeffreys) 3. Break This Fool (Fiddler / Watts) 4. International Heroes (Kim Fowley / Kerry Scott) 5. Fork Talking Man (Fiddler)
Side Two: 1. My Life In Your Hands (Fiddler / Fisher / Watts) 2. Big Drift Away (Fiddler) 3. Booster (Fiddler / Watts) 4. Eat The Rich (Fiddler)

As with the Nigel Benjamin-fronted Mott albums, opinions then and now on the first British Lions album are sharply polarised. Some heralded it as something of a return to form, speculating on how much more successful the band might've been if only John Fiddler had joined in 1975 instead; others saying the album tried to be all things to everyone – punk or post-punk, prog rock and hard rock – sounded bland, directionless, and compared poorly with the old band. Appreciated for what it is without any preconceptions over Ian Hunter moving on, it's an enjoyable, varied set that had the misfortune of being out of its time in Britain and thus was unfairly ignored.

John's song 'One More Chance To Run' made an excellent first track and debut single. A crunching rhythm guitar intro, a genuine chorus hook (the likes of which usually eluded Overend in his songs), a slower bridge before the last chorus, and Morgan's sparkling keyboard runs, all mark this out as a bit of a blinder. It's also evident that John – previously identified with the more laid-back Medicine Head style – has discovered an inner voice that really rocks out. 'Break This Fool' straddles hard rock, with a scorching guitar riff and punchy keyboards, while the Bo Diddley rhythm of 'Fork Talking Man' builds into an impassioned chorus, Morgan adding some neat jazz runs on the keys.

Side two's first two songs veer off more into the realms of prog rock – 'My Life In Your Hands' being especially notable for Ray's lead breaks, while the eight-minute epic 'Big Drift Away' is filled with light and shade, portentous piano and synth effects and another spine-tingling guitar break. In contrast, 'Booster' with its call-and-respond vocals is almost punky, while 'Eat The Rich' – again, with a dose of new wave – is a bit of a joke, as the title suggests, but it *is* cleverly done. After the first few seconds of – as it says on the inner bag, Morgan eating, and – tinkling glockenspiel, the opening line 'Authority stinks' suggests where it's going, and a strong chorus rounds it off.

Of the two cover songs, Garland Jeffreys' 'Wild In The Streets' was one they'd demoed with Steve Hyams, but the British Lions recording leaves that earlier one at the starting gate. Kim Fowley and Kerry Scott's 'International Heroes' – more or less a power ballad – has a hint of 'All The Young Dudes' about it, and had been under consideration for recording by the old Ian-led band. Ray's stylish guitar intro and some delightfully bombastic synth work, mark this one out.

On the first listen or two, the album may sound a little too eclectic and everything-but-the-kitchen-sink, but scratch deeper and it's very good, well played and with a healthy dose of humour. It was certainly not mired in early-1970s styles. Much of this was down to Morgan, who tried to get them all thinking *new wave*; bringing them new records and asking what they thought; going out to clubs regularly to hear punk bands and absorb something of the vibe.

From January to June, British Lions had a full date sheet at home, playing several gigs a week, with an enforced break in early May when some shows were cancelled due to John losing his voice. He said he'd never been in a five-piece rock and roll band before, and after the more bluesy, laid-back Medicine Head, it was tremendously exciting. On some

shows, British Lions were headlining, and on others, they supported AC/
DC or Judas Priest. AC/DC were especially good to work with, and the
Lions were very impressed with their front-of-house sound.

Neither 'One More Chance To Run' (which was released in a picture
bag) nor the second single 'International Heroes' (which was not) ever
featured on the Radio 1 daytime playlist, but they *did* receive an airing
on John Peel's late evening show – in a period when he was the BBC's
punk champion yet still featured records from early-1970s rock acts
as part of what he called his review function, as Peel said later 'with a
disgraceful display of truculence on my part'. They also recorded a Peel
session on 10 May, consisting of 'One More Chance to Run', 'Break This
Fool' and 'Wild In The Streets', broadcast twelve days later. John Peel had
been a passionate Medicine Head fan and supporter, signing them to his
Dandelion label, which had its sole chart entry in 1971 courtesy of their
third single '(And The) Pictures In The Sky'. Dale thought that Peel never
really took to the Lions but included them on his show anyway as he still
had some loyalty to John Fiddler.

In June, British Lions played a 50-minute set on Musikladen TV in
Germany. For Morgan, it was the occasion when he donned makeup to
look unshaven, smeared it over his face in the closing number 'Eat the
Rich', and – fortified by good white wine – ended up throwing potted
palms around.

It was obvious that sales and subsequent chart action would probably
elude them in Britain, and it did. They'd always been aware that their best
hope lay on the other side of the Atlantic – where media and fans were
more open-minded and receptive to anyone over 30 and where it was not
necessary to be a fully-paid-up punk rocker. Knowing they were *too old*
and lacking in street cred for a new band in Britain, the band recognised
they were tailor-made for the USA. Their journey westwards was rendered
more convivial when they learned that the promised movie cassettes had
not been loaded aboard the flight. So in lieu of this and by way of apology,
there would be free drinks for all on the plane. It was naturally an offer
too good to refuse, and by the time they landed, Morgan and John –
who'd never been to America – were happily inebriated.

Thanks to the initial combination of good RSO promotion bringing
subsequent interest and radio exposure in America, the album entered
the *Billboard* charts at the end of April: before the band had even set foot
there. Starting on 12 July at Johnstown, Pennsylvania, they toured America
for almost three months, supporting a variety of British and American

acts, including Blue Oyster Cult, UFO, Cheap Trick, Dr. Hook and Alvin Lee. UFO guitarist Michael Schenker loved British Lions so much after seeing them that he said he wanted to join. As he was one of the great guitar gods of the era, they were flattered, though they had no intention of replacing Ray. Moreover, Michael was well-known as something of a loose cannon with a penchant for walking off-stage during UFO shows without warning, so adding him to the lineup would've been a mixed blessing at best.

The *British Lions* album enjoyed a 14-week American chart run, while 'Wild In The Streets' was extracted as a single in July and spent four weeks in the chart, reaching a high of 87. Their setlist was built solidly around the album, with no songs from Medicine Head or either phase of Mott's back catalogue – except for 'Love Now' from *Drive On*, which they introduced as a song by their previous band The Concrete Parachutes. 'Come On' remained, and they also included an eight-minute medley arranged by Morgan – featuring 'So You Want To Be A Rock 'n' Roll Star' and the opening riff from 'Jumpin' Jack Flash' – then slipping seamlessly into 'It's Only Rock 'N Roll (But I Like It)', and 'Pretty Vacant'. Morgan said they approved wholeheartedly of the whole punk rock movement, even if the punk fans thought differently about *them*, and they were proud to play a Sex Pistols song for American audiences who might otherwise never have heard a proper British punk song on stage. The Americans also accepted British Lions as a new band in their own right, with no audience members calling out for 'All The Way From Memphis', except in Memphis itself. A few critics grumbled that they weren't Mott The Hoople, which pleased the band greatly. They insisted they were not *meant* to be Mott The Hoople.

The American gigs were an undoubted success – selling out, garnering positive reviews, the band going down a storm everywhere they played as they sharpened up the songs and stage act all the time. There was inevitably the occasional hair-raising incident during their stay, such as when a rather drunken Morgan decided on the spur of the moment to walk on stage at New York club Max's Kansas City while punk band The Rippers were playing, so he could help out on keyboards. It ended in a fight with verbal threats of immediate death and Morgan throwing the keyboards all over the stage before being hastily rescued. The Rippers were duly apologetic when they found out who this uninvited intruder was, and a cheery after-show party including both bands and assorted hangers-on was thrown in John's hotel room – briefly interrupted by a contingent of cops who realised that some of the punk band's entourage had been smoking dope, but they left without making any arrests.

Another incident was averted when during the set opener 'One More Chance To Run', John's guitar failed to produce any sound. In frustration, he threw the instrument down in the direction of the audience, and only afterwards realised that it might've hit somebody, with potentially serious consequences. Fortunately, one of the roadies had the foresight to intercept it before any injuries resulted. Later on, in the same gig, John became really angry and started throwing mike stands around the stage, but again without anyone getting hurt.

Several live recordings were made, some released on CD many years later, testifying to what a tight performance they delivered night after night without fail. One of these was at San Francisco's Old Waldorf at the beginning of September, and was broadcast live on local radio. It testifies to the way the band improvised on stage – Morgan adding a snatch of 'Strangers In The Night' to his 'Break This Fool' solo and a few bars of Beethoven's 'Moonlight Sonata' (sic) to 'Eat The Rich'.

Only one vital ingredient was missing on the tour: gigs in major cities. They were playing the secondary markets, the B-list territory. Appearances in New York, Chicago, Boston, Philadelphia and the like were essential if British Lions were to break through as a major act. RSO was then enjoying phenomenal American success, The Bee Gees plus the *Saturday Night Fever* and *Grease* soundtrack albums dominating the charts on a scale that almost echoed that of The Beatles' 1964 invasion – and could easily afford a little extra promotional spending. At the schedule's conclusion, the Lions were booked for two gigs at Hollywood's Starwood Club – one of them attended by the RSO suits, who were less than impressed. The band were certain that a few dates in some of the big cities would give them the final push they needed, and possibly even drive the album into the top ten. Instead, they were told there was no chance of the tour being extended, and they were to go back to England and record a second album. They flew home: some of them to find their personal lives in turmoil. The phrase 'Trouble With Women' – the title of a new song John wrote to kick-start the second album – summed it all up.

The band spent several weeks at RAK Studios from November 1978 to January 1979, laying down that song and seven more in the most difficult of circumstances. There was little material to start with, though John and Overend had some ideas to develop, soon coming up with finished songs to arrange and rehearse. Yet they had no money between them, and morale was at an all-time low. Morgan needed to pay his mortgage, and as a session musician, he could still find ready employment, so he spent part of the time working with John Otway on his forthcoming album *Where Did I Go Right?* Ray was in hospital for a while with hepatitis, so Bruce Irvine stepped in on guitar for one track, Overend contributing to three, until Ray was fit enough to resume duties. On some days, only one band member was coming to the studio. Overend remarked it was 'absolute hell', with 'no kind of atmosphere to be productive'.

Chapter Ten: 1979-1980

British Lions completed recording and mixing their second and last album in January 1979. But none of them could pretend it had been a productive experience.

In Morgan's elegant phrase, 'RSO and then Phonogram, in a display of unswerving loyalty, gave us the pink slip after the (first) album had failed to go gold'. Dale was a little more explicit, saying that RSO didn't like the follow-up because it sounded 'too cold and bleak', and demanded changes. At a meeting with Colin Johnson, he told them that Phonogram in London were less negative, but wanted four tracks removed and replaced, one of them being 'Electric Chair'. Moreover, as had happened to Mott The Hoople in 1972, the band were told they could carry on as before, but in downsized form with greatly reduced pay, crew, sound and lights, and needed to build up a home fan base with an endless slogging round the pubs and smaller clubs. When Colin said he had a gig list prepared – noting places they'd gone down well before and naming some of the small venues – the band told him that they were not going back there. He wanted them to see the group as a long-term venture – doing what Status Quo had done in Britain at the start of the decade: gradually working their way up from the bottom.

John and Ray were prepared to say yes, and Morgan was in two minds. But Dale and Overend had had more than enough in the last ten or fifteen years of trying to make a living with the fates repeatedly conspiring against them – *and* they still owed the taxman several thousand pounds. Did Overend ever regret not having accepted the offer from Peter Grant and Bad Company or The Bee Gees? They believed that the only thing that would turn the situation around was a really long American tour to capitalise on the previous year's groundwork. When management firmly ruled this out, the drummer and bassist announced they were leaving, and British Lions simply ceased to exist. Morgan thought it had been a wasted opportunity. They went down really well almost everywhere they played, and it was soul-destroying when management and record company did virtually nothing in return and refused to listen to their ideas.

As their former frontman had once observed in song, 'Rock 'n' roll's a loser's game'. Dale and Stan Tippins got in touch with Ian around this time to broach the possibility of working together again. He said that as much as he liked and respected them all, he'd rather keep Mott The Hoople as a souvenir, and a reunion would mean nothing.

Trouble With Women *(British Lions) (1980)*

Personnel:

John Fiddler: vocals, guitar, harmonica

Ray Major: lead guitar, vocals

Morgan Fisher: keyboards, vocals

Overend Watts: bass, guitar, vocals

Dale Griffin: drums, vocals

Bruce Irvine: guitar

Producer: British Lions

Studio: RAK, London, November 1978-January 1979

Release date: June 1980

Chart placings: UK: -, US: -

Running time: 34:26

Side One: 1. Trouble With Women (Fiddler) 2. Any Port In A Storm (Fiddler) 3. Lady Don't Fall Backwards (Watts / Fiddler) 4. High Noon (Fisher / Fiddler) Side Two: 1. Lay Down Your Love (Watts / Fiddler) 2. Waves Of Love (Watts / Fiddler) 3. Electric Chair (Fiddler) 8. Won't You Give Him One (More Chance) (Bobby Scott / Angela Martin)

Trouble With Women was recorded quickly, under pressure and in very trying circumstances. None of the group had good memories of the sessions, and in subsequent interviews some years later, they made no effort to pretend that they liked it. The then-newly-established indie label Cherry Red acquiring and releasing the album about eighteen months after its completion, passed almost unnoticed, and most retrospective reviews online are as dismissive as the original reviews were. There's little denying that the record lacks the sense of adventure, excitement and occasional eccentricity that still makes the first album such a joy. Which track would've made the best single? Nobody ever got as far as needing to decide, but there was nothing to hit the listener with the sheer force that the first album's 'One More Chance To Run' had. Even gifted songwriter John – who wrote three songs and co-penned four others – wilted under the pressure of having to quickly come up with anything as strong after having been on the road for so long.

The title track hints at a funk influence – something many bands experimented with at the end of the 1970s, with varying success. Based partly on guitar chords bearing some similarity to Them's 'Gloria', the band pause briefly about halfway through for a few seconds of harmonica and bass, before ending in a startling flurry of feedback. Nothing special at first, repeated listens reveal it to be quite an inventive piece after all.

'Any Port In A Storm' has the benefit of atmospheric guitar, piano and stormy sound effects, while Byrds-like jangling guitar introduces the more poppy 'Lady Don't Fall Backwards', which has a healthy dose of organ and a brief snippet of comedian Tony Hancock – the song title being taken from 'The Missing Page': a 1960 episode of his TV show *Hancock's Half-Hour* concerning a fictitious murder-mystery novel. This and the slower 'High Noon', with its grungy guitar and organ, are the two tracks that feature Morgan most strongly – his input on the album as a whole being missed on other tracks.

Side two has its good moments, though overall sounds less inspired. 'Lay Down Your Love' succeeds in the guitar solo department, and boasts some nifty bass soloing, 'Waves Of Love' looks forward to electropop: particularly on the intro, while the brooding 'Electric Chair' is a dark, slow and menacing number with pungent guitar.

To finish off, a cover of the mid-1960s song 'Won't You Give Him One (More Chance)' (that The Silence had performed) – best remembered in versions by The T-Bones and Solomon Burke – is pleasant enough and moderately commercial, but sounds too lightweight for a group of the Lions' calibre. It was a sadly anti-climactic note on which to end a short recording career that had shown so much promise.

Ian's association with Chrysalis via Generation X proved to be as productive as he'd hoped, enabling him to secure a new deal with the label. At last, he was able to resume his partnership with Mick Ronson, resulting in the album that many regard as the best of Ian's solo career.

Before starting the sessions, both men agreed that in order to keep the music fresh, they had to change things. Mick's previous management contract had guaranteed him more money from Ian's records than Ian was earning himself: a state of affairs that was obviously untenable between friends. When that ended, the air cleared between them, and Ian signing to Chrysalis clearly signified a new start.

The new album's original working title was *The Outsider*, after the song Ian had introduced on the sessions with Corky Laing the previous year. The album title was later changed to *You're Never Alone With A Schizophrenic*, which Mick had seen scrawled on a toilet wall in New York. Ian loved the title, and when Mick allowed him to use it, Ian rewarded him with a co-writer credit on the album's first single, 'Just Another Night'.

The original album sessions began in October 1978 at Wessex Sound Studios with bassist Glen Matlock, drummer Clive Bunker and engineer

Bill Price. Glen already knew Mick from him producing and played keyboards on the first (and only) album by Rich Kids: the group Glen formed with Midge Ure after leaving the Sex Pistols. Glen was out at Covent Garden one evening with Mick, when Ian appeared, saying that what he really needed was a 'safety-pin band'. Over a few days, they recorded rough versions of about half a dozen tracks (Glen said afterwards that he thought they'd tried to get Simon Kirke in on drums), but the songs were nowhere near ready. Glen told Ian he was wasting money by working things out during expensive studio time, and he should go home and finish the songs first. Ian took the advice, and that was the end of the team's involvement and their sessions.

Steve Popovich – former senior A&R man at Epic Records and then founder and head of Cleveland International Records – played the demos to Bruce Springsteen's pianist Roy Bittan. As the E Street Band were available, Steve rang Ian and suggested he and Mick come and record in New York. They were on the next plane.

You're Never Alone With A Schizophrenic *(Ian Hunter)(1979)*

Personnel:
Ian Hunter: vocals, guitar, piano, Moog, ARP, organ, percussion
Mick Ronson: vocals, guitar, percussion
Roy Bittan: ARP, organ, Moog, piano, vocals
Max Weinberg: drums
Garry Tallent: bass
John Cale: piano, ARP
George Young: tenor saxophone
Lew Delgatto: baritone saxophone
Ellen Foley, Rory Dodd, Eric Bloom: backing vocals
Producers: Mick Ronson, Ian Hunter
Studio: The Power Station, New York, January 1979
Release date: March 1979
Chart placings: UK: 49, US: 35
Running time: 42:04
All songs written by Ian Hunter unless stated otherwise
Side One: 1. Just Another Night (Hunter / Mick Ronson) 2. Wild East 3. Cleveland Rocks 4. Ships 5. When The Daylight Comes
Side Two: 1. Life After Death 2. Standin' In My Light 3. Bastard 4. The Outsider
Bonus tracks, 30th anniversary 2005 reissue
10. Don't Let Go (Demo) 11. Ships (Take 1) 12. When The Daylight Comes (Early

version) 13. The Other Side Of Life (Early version of 'When The Daylight Comes')
14. Whole Lotta Shakin' Goin' On (Curly Williams / Sunny David)
A second disc includes fifteen tracks recorded live on tour between June and
November 1979 in Cleveland, London, and at Berkeley, California.

You're Never Alone With A Schizophrenic was split in two, with the rockers and a ballad on side one, and four longer, more introspective songs on the other. It features an all-star backing group of E Street Band members Roy Bittan, Garry Tallent and Max Weinberg, and backing vocalists Rory Dodd, Ellen Foley, and Eric Bloom of Blue Oyster Cult.

'Just Another Night' was originally a ballad with the title 'The Other Side Of Life'. When Ian played it for Mick Ronson, he said it needed to be a rocker, and it does get the album off to a crisp start with its heavy rhythm and pounding piano. The lyrics were inspired by a night Ian spent in jail in Indianapolis on the 1973 American tour. After an incident in a hotel, he fell foul of the management, one of whom was an off-duty sergeant.

'Just Another Night' always went down well on stage. Roy Bittan had worked out what Ian recognised was a more commercial arrangement, which was good, though it sounded too much like a Bruce Springsteen track. Ian had nothing against the man he called 'the mighty Bruce', but despite what Roy advised, he didn't want a hit that sounded like somebody else.

'Wild East' is the song on which Roy Bittan, Garry Tallent and Max Weinberg of the E Street Band shine – Max giving Ian what he later said was the best drum sound he'd ever heard. The lyric suggests a love/hate relationship with aspects of the American lifestyle, as he ponders how watching TV is killing him: 'It's such a drag tonight/I feel like Jason just found a rusty fleece'.

The two-year-old single 'England Rocks' appears with a respray job as 'Cleveland Rocks' – Ian's defence of the condition of Cleveland, and going back to early Mott days when the city was considered much less cool than New York or LA. With a bubbling synth at times recalling The Who's 'Won't Get Fooled Again', the intro references its inspiration with a snatch of pioneering American DJ Alan Freed, aka Moondog introducing his show from the early days of rock and roll radio. Being another regular concert crowd-pleaser, the song received a new lease of life in 1997 when The Presidents of the United States of America covered it as the opening theme for the American sitcom *The Drew Carey Show*, though it wasn't released as a single.

'Ships' – the album's first ballad – is, without doubt, one of Ian's best. It's a melancholy keyboard-driven song with discreet backing vocals put to good use. The lyric was inspired by the often distant relationship Ian had with his father. They were direct opposites – the usual generation-gap saga – with Mr. Patterson never really understanding or taking to his son's music, but he was proud when Ian published *Diary of a Rock'n'Roll Star* in 1974 and it proved to be a literary success. Ian's father died two years after *You're Never Alone With A Schizophrenic* was released, and Ian was thankful his father had a chance to hear and appreciate the song. With its opening memories of walking along the seashore as a boy with his father and the lines 'We're two ships that pass in the night/And we smile when we say 'It's alright'', it's an almost misty-eyed recollection of how kith and kin can be so different but – blood being thicker than water – always retain a certain closeness.

Ian was initially dissatisfied with the song when in progress, but his managers made him finish it. His efforts were rewarded when the head of Arista, Clive Davis, played it to Barry Manilow and recommended that he cover it. Barry, who had recently lost his father, recorded it for his next album *One Voice,* retaining the arrangement, and it became a top-10 hit in America later that year. Before recording it, he rang Ian to ask if he could write some different lines for the bridge. Ian considered it but never got round to doing so on the grounds that once a song was released, he considered it to effectively be in the public domain.

'When The Daylight Comes' is another solid mid-tempo rocker, soulful and organ-driven with rousing guitar riffs and vulnerable lyrics about romance. Mick sang the first two verses. Ian was busy talking to Bruce Springsteen in the studio – Mick urged him to come and sing it, and Ian said to hang on a minute. Mick's response was 'Come and do it now, or I'll do it!', and he did.

On side two, portentous, spacey synth effects and a subtle guitar solo serve as an intro for the questioning 'Life After Death'. For the first few seconds, Ian's voice sounds like it's coming from the bottom of a deep chasm, if not another universe entirely. The drums then launch the song itself. The lyric hints eerily at confronting the Grim Reaper, with lines like 'I hear choirs filled with Fenders say return to sender' and 'Jumping information, I've got hyperventilation'. When asked what the lyric was about, Ian simply replied, 'It's just fun, and fear'.

The album's most ethereal number, 'Standin' In My Light,' came about from Ian finding a keyboard sound and writing something around it.

The subject matter was inspired by his dealings with Tony DeFries, and is basically a weary lyric about having had enough of being overshadowed by people who fail to meet expectations. It includes the line 'Ain't gonna trade with the pain of the New York Dolls', as he resented the attention they were getting, 'because they lacked substance'.

At first glance, 'Bastard' could've been taken as a riposte to bad management, but Ian insisted it was 'a truthful love song, as opposed to all the dreck'. He said there were millions of love songs and they all say the same things. This was his effort at looking beyond sentimentality and trying to be more realistic. A sinister seething rocker, it features John Cale on piano and synthesizer, as the song has 'that eerie, ominous thing that he can do so well'.

To close, comes 'The Outsider'. The six-minute-long ballad epic is the weary lament of a man on life's margins: 'When the wind grows cold, when the sun grows old/Nothing holds the outsider'. After a subdued two-minute opening, the drums kick in, with swirling guitar and keyboards, and a scorching guitar solo as the final moments.

Taken as a whole, the album doesn't immediately fit into the 'radio-friendly and commercial-yet-bordering-on-hard-rock' bracket as easily as the 1975 solo debut did. Nevertheless, critics hailed it as a positive return to form – and after its creator's dissatisfaction with his previous two projects (which he felt had come close to killing his career), it convinced him that he was back on the right track. It was the only American top-40 album of Ian's career (with 'Just Another Night' the only top-100 single), and more than forty years later is regarded as his best solo work. Upon its release, *Record Mirror* called it 'By far the strongest, most consistent album' he'd released since Mott The Hoople split.

In Britain, Chrysalis issued three singles from the album – 'When The Daylight Comes' in April, on a choice of black or white vinyl; 'Ships' in August, and 'Cleveland Rocks' in November, but none of them charted. 'Just Another Night' reached 68 in America. Ian and Mick toured there to promote the album, playing several dates from June to the beginning of September. With the E Street Band unavailable, they put together a touring outfit consisting of guitarist Tommy Morrongiello, bassist Martin Briley, keyboadist Tommy Mandel, drummer Hilly Michaels and keyboardist/saxophonist George Meyer. Most of the musicians also appeared on Ellen Foley's Ronson/Hunter-produced debut album *Night Out* released in June. That included a new Ian song called 'Don't Let Go', on which he and Mick played.

Chrysalis was thrilled that one of their latest acquisitions had come up trumps, and wanted a second album as soon as possible. As he rarely wrote while on the road, Ian had few new songs ready and did not intend to be rushed into a sub-standard follow-up. When the label suggested a live album with one side of new material recorded live in the studio, Ian was initially reluctant, as he preferred to record a completely new project. But the label was keen to capitalise on him while he was hot. Seven nights were booked at the Roxy in Hollywood from 5 to 11 November, and all quickly sold out. They were recorded for a live set that was initially to be titled *From the Knees of my Heart*. Comedian Billy Connolly was booked as the support act, but left after the first night because the audience wouldn't listen to him and kept talking and drinking throughout his act. Another star who had a problem with the show was Sonny Bono's former wife Cher, who walked out after the band played 'Laugh At Me'.

After the American dates, they took the show to London. Ian and Mick made an appearance at Our Price Records in Kensington, signing albums and photos. Steve Hyams was among those who went to meet them, and they went for lunch afterwards. The following night, the band played at Hammersmith Odeon, where the gig was recorded; later edited for broadcast on Radio 1's *In Concert* series. While in London, Ian appeared on Radio 1's *Roundtable* with David 'Kid' Jensen, talking about the week's new releases. Ian also recorded a two-hour *Star Special* for broadcast on the same station several months later – playing a personal selection of music from artists including Little Richard, Jerry Lee Lewis, The Beatles, The Rolling Stones and Wizzard.

At the beginning of 1980, fans had a choice of two double albums to choose from. In February – wise to Ian's renaissance on Chrysalis – CBS delivered *Shades of Ian Hunter*: the first of a long line of compilation albums combining his group and solo work. One set contained Mott The Hoople's singles (except 'Honaloochie Boogie'), B-sides and a few album tracks; the second had material from Ian's solo career, with the final side devoted to *Overnight Angels* numbers. The only previously unavailable cut was a live version of 'Marionette' from the Broadway show in May 1974.

Chrysalis had been ready to issue their live set in March but held it back until the beginning of April to avoid following the CBS one too soon. Now titled *Welcome to the Club*, it contained fourteen live numbers over three sides, with four live-in-the-studio cuts on side four.

Welcome to the Club *(Ian Hunter)* *(1980)*
Personnel:
Ian Hunter: vocals, rhythm guitar, piano, harmonica
Mick Ronson: vocals, guitar, Moog synthesizer, mandolin
Tommy Morongiello: guitar, vocals
Tommy Mandel: keyboards
Martin Briley: bass
Eric Parker: drums
George Meyer: keyboards, saxophone, vocals
Ellen Foley, Susie Ronson: backing vocals
Live tracks (1-14, 18) recorded 5-11 November 1979 at the Roxy Theatre, Hollywood.
Live-in-studio tracks (15-17) recorded 10-11 January 1980 at Media Sound, New York City.
Producer: Ian Hunter
Release date: 26 March 1980
Chart placings: UK: 61, US: 69
Running time: 88:07
All songs written by Ian Hunter unless stated otherwise
Side One: 1. F.B.I. (Hank Marvin / Bruce Welch / Jet Harris) 2. Once Bitten Twice Shy
3. Angeline 4. Laugh At Me (Sonny Bono) 5. All The Way From Memphis
Side Two: 1. I Wish I Was Your Mother 2. Irene Wilde 3. Just Another Night (Hunter / Mick Ronson) 4. Cleveland Rocks
Side Three: 1. Standin' In My Light 2. Bastard 3. Walkin' With a Mountain/Rock And Roll Queen (Hunter / Mick Ralphs) 4. All The Young Dudes (David Bowie)
5. Slaughter On Tenth Avenue (Richard Rodgers)
Side Four: 1. We Gotta Get Out Of Here 2. Silver Needles 3. Man O' War (Hunter / Mick Ronson) 4. Sons And Daughters
Bonus tracks: The 2007 reissue adds four live tracks: one a three-song medley. The second disc of *From The Knees of my Heart* adds two live tracks from the 2007 reissue.

From the moment the compere announces 'The Ian Hunter Band, featuring Mick Ronson', the crowd go wild to the opening strains of 'F.B.I.' – a rocked-up arrangement of the old Shadows instrumental that had been the Hunter/ Ronson band opener for some years. The tune is instantly recognisable for the most part, the exception being the short bridge that Mick added to the arrangement.

Except for a short 'Slaughter On Tenth Avenue', the live numbers are all drawn from Ian's solo catalogue and the Mott The Hoople albums, going back to 'Laugh At Me' (which had displeased Cher), and those other Island-era evergreens 'Angeline' and a medley of 'Walkin' With A Mountain'/'Rock And Roll Queen'. While there are a few slow moments (notably 'I Wish I Was Your Mother' followed by 'Irene Wilde'), it's clearly the rockers that fire the audience up – especially 'Cleveland Rocks', which has them chanting along with a roll call of other American places: Philadelphia, Chicago, San Francisco, New York, and finally 'America rocks'. Sometimes (but not on this version), Ian was known to slip in the words 'Disco sucks' as well.

The four new songs making up side four of the original vinyl release are a suitably varied batch. By Ian's own admission, 'We Gotta Get Out Of Here' 'was a nod to what was going on at the time and a not-too-successful stab at a single', a little reminiscent of a few other ironic 45s that made fun of the disco genre (notably Frank Zappa's 'Dancin' Fool' from 1979). It's set largely to an insistent metronomic rhythm and keyboards, then becoming half dialogue as Ian repeats the title, only for backing vocalist Ellen Foley (representing his partner) to taunt him for being such a drag for wanting to go home and watch the Superbowl, when all she wants to do is have fun and dance the night away. 'We Gotta Get Out Of Here' was released as a single in America – narrowly failing to make the *Billboard* Hot 100 – and as the lead track on a double-pack in Britain, but without success. Disco music clearly did not impress Ian, as he had been to Studio 54 once by invitation – an episode about which he was suitably scathing and would be happy to never repeat. He remarked that Donna Summer 'was the only one to come out of that'.

'Silver Needles' enters more serious waters – a plaintive country-ish ballad with a synthetic steel-guitar-like sound prominent throughout. Anger is suffused with sadness and regret about the hard-drug culture and the waste of life for those involved. One moment Ian's almost shouting the words in fury, then his voice falls to a tone of weary resignation. When he wrote it, he had two people in mind – guitarist Tommy Bolin (for whom he'd once signed a copy of his book, and who had succumbed to an overdose in 1976), and even more particularly Sid Vicious, who went down the same destructive path two years later.

There's no message in the lyrics of 'Man O'War' – it's just an unashamedly but perhaps tongue-in-cheek bad-boy number aping The Rolling Stones at their most wilfully misogynistic. If Chrysalis hadn't felt that it had 'unsuitable airplay lyrics', it might've been a single. The guitar sounds like a very good Keith Richards imitation. Ian admitted that neither he nor Mick were keen on the song, as it was put together at the last minute.

The final new song, 'Sons And Daughters' is a bittersweet country waltz following on from where the *Wildlife* track 'Waterlow' left off – and again, clearly written from the heart. Here Ian looks back with sadness on his early married days when he and his wife rented rooms at the Archway (being for an American audience, he sings that the rent was a *dollar* a day, though in London it would've been pounds), and how she 'was a good woman, but the love disappeared'. He tells of finding a band and going out on tour. His children ask where he is, and she tells them their dad is a star – Ian expressing how he hopes they can cope with the damage he's done when a marriage breaks up:

Oh if only stars knew what fools they all are

Sons and daughters, daughters and sons
When a marriage goes down, they're the loneliest ones

Like *You're Never Alone with a Schizophrenic*, *Welcome to the Club* went down well with critics on both sides of the Atlantic. *Melody Maker* praised 'the work of a man of substance', singling out 'Silver Needles' as 'an older (and wiser) man's view' of Sid's death. True to form, *NME* was less sympathetic in its appraisal of the album made up mostly of what it called 'bloated and bombastic' live recordings, but did acknowledge that 'Sons And Daughters' sat with Ian's best work, as a confessional work 'that escapes sounding mawkish, because of the quiet strength of Hunter's delivery and his unwillingness to blame others for the consequences of his own actions'.

Postscript: It's a mighty long way down rock 'n' roll

At the beginning of the 1980s, Ian Hunter was on a roll. As a soloist, he'd made one gem of a solo album, followed by two that were less well-received and almost stalled his career. Now, he'd taken stock. While he never quite scaled the heights that seemed within his grasp at the time of his renaissance with *You're Never Alone with a Schizophrenic* and *Welcome to the Club*, his next two studio albums went down well with the music press but achieved less commercial success. In 1981 he began working on the first of these, to be called *Theatre of the Absurd*. He and Mick Ronson invited Clash guitarist Mick Jones to assist with the title track. Jones had always been a devoted admirer, later saying that if there had been no Mott, there would never have been The Clash, 'nor no me anyway'.

Once the sessions started, Jones was so enthused that he stayed on board for the entire album. Renamed *Short Back 'n' Sides*, it also included participation from Clash drummer Topper Headon, Todd Rundgren and Ellen Foley. Among the tracks were 'Lisa Likes Rock N' Roll' – a song recorded for Mick's small daughter – and 'Old Records Never Die': first recorded on the night of John Lennon's murder in December 1980. Released that summer, the album made a modest showing in the charts on both sides of the Atlantic, reaching 62 in America and 79 in Britain. Ian called it his 'garage' album, and was pleased with the result, adding that Chrysalis hated it. Hindsight and general critical opinion several decades later suggest it was one of Ian's less worthy efforts.

At the time it was released, Ian was mourning the loss of the man who gave him such faith in himself. Guy Stevens had been on a downward spiral for several years, although he had one last triumph in 1979 when he produced the Clash's *London Calling*: recognised as one of the best albums to come out of the punk genre. In August 1981, he overdosed on drugs prescribed to reduce alcohol dependency and died from a heart attack, aged only 38.

Ian had another busy live schedule throughout the year – with three shows in mainland Europe in April and more than twenty in June, most of them supporting Heart. In August, he played three more European shows, two of them in England on one day – the first, supporting Thin Lizzy at the Milton Keynes Festival in the afternoon. He met the headliners, got on very well with them, and an obliging Phil Lynott acted as babysitter so Ian's wife Trudi could watch some of the show. That evening, Ian and his band played a late show at the 101 Club in London.

For artist and label, there would then be another parting of the ways. After a former liaison man Dick Asher rejoined CBS/Columbia, Ian signed to the company again. In the winter of 1982, he began the album *All of the Good Ones are Taken* – co-produced with British producer Max Norman, best known for his work with Ozzy Osbourne. Mick Ronson was seriously considering leaving the music business and only appeared on the track 'Death Or Glory Boys' – Ian's trenchant comment on the Falklands war of the previous year, which he said 'should never have happened'.

Other artists appearing on the record included E Street Band saxophonist Clarence Clemons on the title track, Dan Hartman on bass, and Eric Troyer and Rory Dodd on backing vocals. Ian claimed that Columbia did nothing to promote it, but 'shoved it out the back door as if they were embarrassed', and it charted at 125 in America but bombed in Britain. Nevertheless, there would be two cover versions of songs from the album, with The Monkees recording 'Every Step Of The Way' and Status Quo 'Speechless'.

It would be Ian's last release of the 1980s. He built a home studio, where he continued to write and record demos, but for him and Mick Ronson, much of the decade proved to be a musical wasteland. It was a time when they both lost themselves, hating the period that to them was dominated by what he called 'the corporate-takeover bands with hair extensions and lipstick'. Commercially, they realised they couldn't compete with the top-selling names, and though they did some production projects together, they avoided it much of the time, as they found they were 'lumbered with people who couldn't play'. Ian said everyone has a period where 'things go off the rails in their life', and this was his. After a New York gig in July 1982, he didn't play live again until October 1986, having remained out of sight during the mid-decade Live Aid era.

At length, the muse struck again, one reason being that Trudi had enough of him lying on the bed watching MTV, moaning about how dire everything was, asking him why he didn't get out and do something himself. So Ian and Mick toured Canada with The Roy Young Band, and The Hunter Ronson Band gradually took shape.

Much of 1988 and 1989 was spent touring North America, Britain and Europe. A deal with PolyGram followed, and they recorded a new album at the Power Station, New York. Originally to be called *American Music*, it later became *YUI Orta*, after the Three Stooges catchphrase 'Why you,

I oughta ...'. Released in America in October 1989, and in Britain three months later on the Mercury label, it received favourable reviews but only reached 157 stateside and didn't chart in the UK. Despite being dropped by PolyGram, Ian and Mick were eager to record a follow-up, but plans came to nothing when Mick was diagnosed with liver cancer.

In April 1992, an all-star concert was held at Wembley Stadium as a tribute to Freddie Mercury, who'd died from AIDS the previous November. A host of names appeared with Queen that day, among them Ian and an ailing Mick, making his last high-profile live appearance. Ian and Mick led a performance of 'All The Young Dudes', joined by Queen, David Bowie and Def Leppard members Joe Elliott and Phil Collen. Mick passed away exactly one year later, aged 46. The two men had been musical brothers for almost 20 years, and it was the end of a chapter in Ian's life. It hit him hard, and for a while, he became reclusive, not really wanting to get involved in anything. Later he admitted that Mick's death gave him a wake-up call and motivated him to return to work. *The Artful Dodger* – released in Norway in 1996 and in Britain a year later – included the tribute 'Michael Picasso'.

A full schedule of further albums and tours followed over the next few years. His next album – *Rant* in 2001 – was his most fiercely political for many years. The particularly incisive 'Death Of A Nation' lambasted the politicians Ian held responsible for England's recent decline. Six years later, his next album *Shrunken Heads* took similar aim at the contemporary state of his *adopted* country, with songs like 'Soul Of America' pouring scorn on modern leaders and government corruption.

In 2001, Ian became one of the select fraternity of major rock stars invited to tour America as part of the revolving door of players that was Ringo Starr and His All-Starr Band, playing 26 dates from July to September. Ian had never met any of The Beatles but knew such a tour would be interesting to do. The players joining Ian that year were Greg Lake, Howard Jones and Supertramp's Roger Hodgson. At most gigs, Ian was allowed three of his own songs, 'Cleveland Rocks', 'Still Love Rock 'n' Roll' from *Rant*, and 'All The Young Dudes', which still always brought the house down. On some dates, he was allowed four numbers, the extra one being 'Irene Wilde'. Ringo really liked the song, asking Ian at soundcheck one day, 'What's that 'Gonna be somebody someday' song?'. Ian was delighted to find that Ringo had such high regard for one of the lesser-known numbers. Ian loved the tour, finding Liverpool's most famous drummer good fun to be with and 'so normal, it's frightening'. It was a novel experience for Ian to be a sideman for once, and, as he remarked, not everybody in the music business got the opportunity to play alongside a Beatle.

Except for a few acoustic shows, most of Ian's other tours of Britain, Europe and America were with The Rant Band: his own ever-changing lineup. In May 2002, there were fifteen British gigs on his Taking The Mick tour, with a six-piece band including Mick Ralphs, plus a 20-piece orchestra. At various times, the players included guitarist Paul Cuddeford, keyboardist Ian Gibbons, Paul Francis or Gus Goad on bass, and ex-Wings drummer Steve Holley. Gus, who was on the 2001/2002 and 2004 jaunts, spoke many years later about the experience. He said Ian and Mick were both lovely people to work with – very friendly and open as individuals. Ian was always driven and fiercely passionate about his music. In rehearsal, he was a little subdued – rather to Gus's surprise – but once the first gig began, he really let rip on stage, as if he'd been saving his voice for the real thing.

The majority of Ian's former colleagues in Mott The Hoople and subsequent bands, continued to work in the music industry, but on a much smaller scale when it came to live music – with the exception of Mick Ralphs, who helped form Bad Company in 1973, none of the others ever achieving anything like the same success. Dale Griffin worked for BBC Radio 1 with John Walters between 1980 and 1995, producing many sessions for the John Peel show – a little ironic, given that Peel had not been very enthusiastic about British Lions – among the most noteworthy being performances by Pulp, Orchestral Manoeuvres in the Dark, Nirvana and The Smashing Pumpkins.

Despite what some of his colleagues might've said to the contrary, Dale always found him reasonable and easy to work with. Dale suggested that maybe the group had turned up late when they were recording their sessions in the early days, or maybe John was just having a bad day. Now he was on the other side of the desk, Dale appreciated that it could not have been easy for anybody to get a good sound out of heavy rock bands in the old Maida Vale studios. He did recall John having been grumpy about Ian wanting to use headphones to record his vocals but duly sent a studio assistant to the very depths of the Maida Vale building, taking some time to return with a set of cans that could've come out of a World War II plane, or been used with a crystal set. The alternative – which Ian clearly didn't want – was to have the backing track played back at a low level on a monitor speaker. Dale did concede, though, that they were never given a playback of the songs, which he thought was out of order. In time, some he worked with found him to be somewhat trying. BBC recording engineer Martin Colley remembered him not taking the sessions seriously and having a short fuse with bands that he found to be unprofessional. He described Dale as 'difficult', and realised Dale didn't like Mick Ronson. When Martin played a joke on Dale by asking a BBC receptionist to put a call through to Mr. Griffin telling him Mr. Ronson was downstairs and would like to see him, Dale angrily walked out of the studio. One day when The Smiths came to record a session, Morrissey was told that Dale would not talk about Mott The Hoople, so Morrissey was warned not to ask.

Although his days in the group had not ended happily, Dale never ceased to love the music of Mott The Hoople, was proud of the catalogue they'd left behind, and always sought ways to 'keep the flame burning'. Their old fans continued to love them, and there would always be new generations of rock-music lovers eager to discover the music for themselves.

Dale helped oversee the release of several important recordings – from the archives, and some album reissues with bonus tracks (mostly on the Angel Air label) – and often took a major role in writing the informative sleeve and booklet notes, revealing a dry sense of humour. One of the most important was *Two Miles From Heaven* – a superlative collection of Mott The Hoople outtakes recorded between 1969 and 1972, with minor additions: first released by Island in 1980, and subsequently on CD by Angel Air in 1992 with two additional tracks. Highlights included a remix of 'Thunderbuck Ram' with minor keyboard additions from Morgan Fisher, who hadn't joined the group until about three years after the original was released. Several songs by Mick Ralphs included 'Little Christine' (recorded for but not used on the debut album), 'Surfin' UK' (which they stressed was 'more Brighton Beach than Malibu') and his poignant 'Until I'm Gone' (the outtake from *Wildlife*, with additional 12-string guitar and piano from Morgan). There were early versions of 'One Of The Boys', 'Black Scorpio' (co-written by Ian and Overend) and an earlier version of 'Momma's Little Jewel', improved with new slide guitar from Ray Major. The second Island single 'Downtown' was added to the CD edition. Instead of side one and side two, the first was named 'Dark Cargo', after a poem by the Barrow Poets that was a favourite of Overend. Side two was called 'Bald At The Station', after Mick had gone to collect a potential Bad Company member from the train for an audition, and saw a man with a guitar case and a huge shiny bald head waiting for him, and quickly turned around again. In their auditions book, they noted, 'Reason for rejection: bald at the station', deciding afterwards that it would make a good title for something.

Angel Air also reissued all the old Island albums in 2003 – again with bonus material, some with full booklet notes – plus several albums by Mott and British Lions containing concert recordings, demos and radio promos. They all testified to continuing interest in the bands, despite their underwhelming chart success.

Overend Watts more or less left the music business as a performer. He and Dale formed Grimtone Productions to share involvement working with and producing records by Slaughter and the Dogs, Department S, Hanoi Rocks and Dumb Blondes. Returning to his native Hereford, Overend ran a successful secondhand shop for several years. He later sold it and took up the hobby of long-distance walking, covered the South West Coast Path, and recounted the experiences in a book: *The Man Who Hated Walking*.

Mick Ralphs continued to enjoy a high profile as guitarist with Bad Company until the original line-up split in 1982, although he rejoined the reformed group in different lineups from 1986 onwards. In 1999, he announced he was giving up touring, largely due to his fear of flying. He made a couple of solo albums, worked with George Harrison, David Gilmour, and Ian again at various times, and formed The Mick Ralphs Blues Band playing classic blues and R&B standards.

Morgan Fisher set up Pipe Music: an independent studio and record label in London. Among his first projects were the ambient album *Slow Music* and the art-punk album *Hybrid Kids*. The latter was notable for including a synth spoof of 'All The Young Dudes' played in the style of a turn-of-the-century palm court orchestra, with scratches included from an old 78 record. When first playing it to the others, he said it was a vintage piece of music that David Bowie had plagiarised before owning up and admitting it was all his own work. He also recorded *Miniatures* – a collection of 51 one-minute-long pieces by Robert Fripp, Robert Wyatt, The Pretenders, Andy Partridge, The Damned, Penguin Cafe Orchestra and others. In 1982 he toured Europe as keyboard player for Queen, which he enjoyed, but said was less fun than Mott because the shows were always so perfect. While admiring Queen's 'consummate professionalism', he missed Mott's 'madness and spontaneity'. Otherwise, he followed a rather different career path, recording mostly ambient work and music for TV commercials and art videos. Moving to Japan in 1985, he built Handmade Studio to work on his own projects and collaborate with Japanese artists: notably Yoko Ono.

Verden Allen had been making new records regularly since leaving Mott The Hoople in 1973 – mostly a succession of solo singles, one with Dale and Overend in 1983, and one with Luther Grosvenor (who had temporarily dropped the Ariel Bender moniker) in 1984. Luther put his music aside for a while but released a solo album in 1996, playing occasional dates with The Ariel Bender Band.

Nigel Benjamin initially planned to leave the music industry after Mott split in 1976, but after a change of heart, he helped form English Assassin. They signed with Arista and recorded an album, but when company boss Clive Davis said it had to be remixed, the band said no and the release was cancelled. He later joined American glam rock band London (not connected with the British punk band of the same name), which included future members of W.A.S.P. and Guns N' Roses among an ever-changing lineup.

John Fiddler reformed Medicine Head, which included Ray Major (later Ray Majors) for a while. Both worked the London club circuit and were also part of Box of Frogs – another revolving door outfit, formed in 1983 and active long enough to record two albums, in 1984 and 1986. With a nucleus made up of Yardbirds members, guest vocalists included Roger Chapman, Graham Parker and Ian Dury, alongside musicians such as Rory Gallagher, Graham Gouldman and Geraint Watkins. Ray's other work included a stint in Freeway – alongside former Status Quo drummer John Coghlan – later becoming Partners in Crime.

An interesting blast from the past came in 1988 Dale received a call from Betty Jeffery. Her husband Paul had been in some of the early-1960s Hereford bands, and their three sons were curious to know what their dad had sounded like in his music days. Dale told her that no recordings existed except for a few of poor sound quality. Nevertheless, it set him thinking, and in June 1989, all the original members of The Soulents/ Silence – including bassist Robert Fisher – convened in a rehearsal room in Acton. Robert's wife Ruby-Jo joined them, and the result was a jam lasting several hours within which happy memories came flooding back. In October 1990 – following much discussion and planning – the party (minus Mrs. Fisher) loaded their instruments and equipment into Rockfield Studios, Monmouth. Their idea was to record the old numbers, plus 'We'll Silence You' – a new song Robert had just written about the group: their equivalent of 'The Ballad Of Mott' – to celebrate the 25th anniversary of their last performance. Over five days, they rehearsed, recorded with a minimum of overdubs, and mixed the songs.

Years without practice had varying effects on the two best-known members. Dale recalled that Overend 'played a blinder', and not having touched guitar much since 1965, was only just starting to warm to the task again when the time came to pack up and go. Dale really needed six months of hard drums practice, yet he'd had none and was left with pain in his hands, wrists and arms. Although they didn't initially intend to release anything commercially, the project – christened *Shotgun Eyes* on Ruby-Jo's suggestion – came out on CD in March 1998 through Angel Air, and included the twelve tracks recorded in Milan 22 years earlier. The master tapes had long since disappeared, but they managed to borrow a virgin copy of the original vinyl from a collector. Everything fitted onto a CD, with The Doc Thomas Group album being renamed *The Italian Job*, released with an informative illustrated 20-page booklet detailing the bands' histories.

Mott The Hoople compilations continued to hit the market on vinyl and then CD at regular intervals: some of higher quality and better-packaged than others. In 1993, Columbia released *The Ballad of Mott: A Retrospective* – a double CD with 33 tracks, including one from each of the Island albums, and four previously unreleased items from the Columbia vaults – a demo from the Dudes sessions: 'Henry And The H-Bomb'; the original version of the almost-B-side 'Lounge Lizzard'; a brief live excerpt from 'American Pie', and an alternate version of 'Through The Looking Glass'. The booklet notes describe the track as Ian's 'attempt to deflate his own grandiose tendencies', as well as an effort to annoy Dan Loggins: the production supervisor who was in the studio at the time. To them, it was 'the profanity take', laced with some post-watershed invective that Ian had added for a joke and strictly for private circulation. He never intended it for release, and was angry when Columbia deemed otherwise. The compilation did, however have a saving grace other than the previously unreleased tracks, in the form of insights from the group's two leading members. Ian was quoted saying what Mick Ralphs told him the previous year:

If someone had told us then what they tell us now, I never would have left ... We never seemed to get it right somehow. We were always pissing somebody off. Now people realise that we were innovators. When you work as hard as we did, you appreciate that.

Mick added:

> We were pre-punk punks. In a way, that was the problem with Mott. We
> were never really in tune with what was going on. I didn't know at the
> time how much influence we had on people.

When it came to poor compilations, K-tel's *The Best of Mott The Hoople*
released three years later, took some beating. Some heavy rock versions of
Mott's hits and originals featured none of the group and were the work of
Danny McCulloch: former bassist with Eric Burdon and The New Animals.
To add insult to injury, the sleeve notes said the compilation included the
last recordings ever made by the dying Mick Ronson. In March 1998, K-tel
were taken to court for supplying goods with a false description and were
fined £8,000 plus £1,488 costs. But it didn't stop the tracks circulating
as Mott The Hoople, usually on compilations. In 2002, the album was
reissued as *I Can't Believe It's Not Mott The Hoople!*, credited this time to
The Trybe.

Fortunately for the more discerning buyer – and for younger fans who
were keen to catch up with records that in some cases were older than
they were – it would soon be possible to obtain almost everything Mott
The Hoople, Ian Hunter and British Lions had ever recorded. Many an
archive search yielded treasure troves of outtakes, old radio sessions
and live recordings that had been carefully stored away. The first major
collection was *All the Young Dudes: The Anthology*. Issued in September
1998 to coincide with the band's first major biography (by Campbell
Devine), the 3-CD digipak longbox compiled 62 tracks consisting of all
the British hits and 37 unreleased songs or alternate versions or mixes.
Among them were early Island outtakes – 'Moonbus (Baby's Got A
Down)', 'It Would Be a Pleasure' and 'Long Red' – and a wealth of early
rarities including one track each from The Buddies, The Doc Thomas
Group and The Shakedown Sound, alongside demos of 'Shakin' All
Over', 'Please Don't Touch' with vocals by Stan Tippins, and Verden's
'Nightmare'. Five tracks by the Nigel-Benjamin-fronted Mott included the
demo of 'Get Rich Quick': the 1976 song that it had been suggested might
turn their ailing fortunes around.

A 2021 Mott The Hoople and Ian Hunter 3-CD compilation in the *Gold*
series, entered the British chart at 33. Its 50 tracks spanned the CBS years
from 1972 to 1983.

In 2018, UMC issued the early-years cream of the crop on *Mental*

Train: The Island Years – a no-effort-spared box containing six CDs, a foldout poster of the group onstage at Croydon, and a hardback book of memorabilia, photographs and a detailed essay on the band's history by author Kris Needs: former editor of *ZigZag*, and a one-time secretary of the band's fan club the Sea Divers. Four of the CDs were Island-album reissues with bonus outtakes, rehearsals and demos etc. At last, fans could hear the full eleven-minute version of 'You Really Got Me', and also a shorter vocal take. The fifth disc – *The Ballads of Mott The Hoople* – included the legendary fragment of 'Like A Rolling Stone'. The sixth was the twelve-track *It's Live and Live Only*. Six tracks were from the Fairfield Halls, Croydon gig – the 1970 live-album-that-never-was, as nearly all the material recorded had long been thought unusable – and the remaining six were from a BBC Radio 1 *In Concert* session recorded in December 1971, compered by Bob Harris.

The original Mott The Hoople CBS albums were reissued on CD with extra tracks and (sometimes) carefully-annotated booklet notes. Also, a box-set of the five CBS studio records appeared in Columbia's 'Original Albums Classics' series in 2009. Chrysalis, having issued the 1979-1981 albums with bonus tracks, overhauled their Ian Hunter back catalogue in 2019 with *From The Knees of my Heart*: a four-disc package including all three albums with bonus tracks (offering different listings from the stand-alone CD reissues). The fourth disc – *Ian Hunter Rocks* – was recorded live in September 1981 at the Dr Pepper Festival in New York City. This disc contained fourteen tracks, four of them medleys, one made up of 'All The Way From Memphis' and 'Honky Tonk Women'.

The box-set to end all box-sets, *Stranded in Reality*, is a mammoth 30-disc (28 CDs and two DVDs) testimony to the industry of Ian Hunter since he began his solo career in 1975. Proper Records issued it in 2016 in a large presentation case, limited to 2500 copies at a cost of £250, with none of the discs exclusive to the collection being made available separately. Most of the solo albums available at the time – from the eponymous 1975 debut onwards – were included with bonus tracks, CD inner sleeves in replica mini-LP sleeves, a booklet, and nine discs of rare and previously unreleased material comprising an acoustic gig, two rarities collections, various live recordings and demos. The DVDs contained promo films, TV appearances and concert clips going back to the mid-1970s. Completing the package was a lavish hardcover book with a biography of Ian's career to date; a track-by-track rundown of all included material; Ian's unfailingly honest opinions, and a replica music paper called *Shades* (with a *Sounds*-style masthead) with reproductions of album and gig reviews from the past forty years. Topping it all off was an *All American Alien Boy*-era lithograph – all copies individually signed by the man himself.

Rumours of a reformed Mott The Hoople had regularly done the rounds since around the time of Guy Stevens' death in August 1981. After appearing at Milton Keynes Festival earlier in the month, Ian, Mick Ralphs, Overend, Dale and Morgan met to discuss a possible reformation, and – perhaps aided by a certain amount of champagne – plans were made to book a recording session at Wessex Studios. At around the same time, they reunited long enough to play a set on a TV show hosted by musician BA Robertson, until the producer asked them to just make it a medley of three of their hits *Stars On 45*-style, to which they replied with a firm no.

Ten years later, Ian fuelled further speculation by telling Scandinavian fans backstage after a gig that the band had signed to a major record label and would soon be recording new material, but it went no further than that. At different times, other members floated the possibility, most of them agreeing that the only lineup that would work would be Ian, Mick, Overend, Dale and Morgan, occasionally suggesting it would be Verden back on organ, with Morgan on other keyboards. If they agreed on anything, it was that a record company, album, tour and – above all – decent finance with no half-measures, would all be prerequisites of any such decision. At one time or other, at least one member said it would never happen. 'What's the point in 'All The Old Dudes'?' asked Dale.

For years, the closest thing to a reunion would be one or two members appearing with Ian's band. On 16 and 17 April 1999, a Mott The Hoople convention was held at the Robin Hood Pub in Bilston near Wolverhampton. Ian and his band performed on both evenings, and during the encore of the second, Ariel and Verden joined them for 'Walkin' With a Mountain'. In 2002, Mick Ralphs toured Britain as part of Ian's band, and when Ian played at the Shepherds Bush Empire in October 2007, Mick and Verden joined him for the encore. In January 2009, it finally became official – all five original Mott The Hoople members would get back together for two concerts at the Hammersmith Apollo that October. When asked why, Ian wrote on his website: 'I can't speak for the others, but I'm doing it just to see what it's like. Short of war, death, famine, etc., it's *on*'. Tickets sold out immediately, so more dates were added, and those tickets were similarly snapped up fast. At that rate, they could probably have announced a fortnight or even a month of dates and still not satisfied demand.

But a note of sadness prefaced the occasion. Dale had recently been unwell, and fellow Herefordshire musician and Pretenders drummer Martin Chambers took his place. Since his teenage days, Chambers had idolised the Mott drummer, and was the perfect choice to step in behind the kit, though Dale did come on for the encores. Mick Wall, when interviewing Mott members by telephone and in person for *Classic Rock*, observed that Dale was 'well-spoken and cheerily obliging', but was also the quietest of them all – 'a stooped and almost stumbling figure'. Mick asked Ian what the man who was in the top ten in 1973 singing 'You gotta stay young, man/You can never grow old' might've said if then told he'd be making a comeback with the group at the age of 70? Ian's response was, 'Oh God! It would have been unimaginable'.

Two warm-up gigs were played at the Blake Theatre, Monmouth on 25 and 26 September, followed by a further rehearsal in London later that week. On 1 October, they walked onstage at Hammersmith, to the taped strains of 'Jupiter', for the first of their five-night stint. 'Hymn For The Dudes' opened the show, followed by 'Rock And Roll Queen'. For the five nights, they delivered a packed set lasting over two hours, with ample representation of the Island and CBS years, but only three songs from the post-Mick Ralphs era – 'Born Late '58' (with Ian on bass so Overend could play guitar and also handle the lead vocal), 'The Golden Age Of Rock 'n' Roll' and 'Saturday Gig'. The following songs all left the audiences delighted – 'One Of The Boys', acoustic versions of 'I Wish I Was Your Mother' and 'Original Mixed-Up Kid', an as-powerful-as-ever 'Walkin' With a Mountain', 'Sweet Angeline', an excerpt from 'Like A Rolling Stone' segueing into 'The Journey', 'Honaloochie Boogie' (discarded from the setlist in early days not long after becoming their second hit), 'All The Way From Memphis', inevitably 'All The Young Dudes' with much singing along, and towards the end, 'Keep A-Knockin''. From the stage, Ian and Mick shook hands with those in the front row, and crowds stood throughout every performance, with Ian claiming it was the first time they'd ever received a standing ovation for a full show.

The broadsheet press reviewed the first night's show favourably – *The Guardian* observing there was something slightly chaotic about the sound, and that one encore threatened to fall apart, 'but the lack of slickness somehow just adds to the appeal'. The *Daily Telegraph* summed it up as 'a dazzling night'. A recording was released on CD and vinyl immediately, it being proclaimed that 'all the audio was mixed live, in real time, nothing added, nothing taken away, 100% pure Mott'.

As far as British audiences were concerned, it would not be the final ballad of Mott. In November 2013 – following Ian's ever-full schedule of dates in America (including two supporting Jethro Tull in June 2010), Britain (among them the Isle of Wight Festival in June 2013) and Europe – the group returned. This time there were five dates – in Birmingham, Glasgow and Newcastle, followed by two at London's O2 Arena. By now, the reviewers were less than uniformly generous. In *The Guardian,* Ian Gittins wrote that Ian's voice was by now 'little more than a guttural rasp', but 'the classic singles shine like diamonds'. Suggestions were made elsewhere that perhaps it was 'a reunion too far'.

The story was still not over. In June and July 2018, three European festival dates in Spain, England and Sweden, were arranged for Mott The Hoople – or more specifically, Ian and the Rant Band, with Ariel Bender and Morgan Fisher joining guitarists James Mastro and Mark Bosch, keyboardist Dennis DiBrizzi, bassist Paul Page and drummer Steve Holley.

Hunter and Ronson had played the first fundraiser for the Rock and Roll Hall of Fame at a ceremony in New York in November 1989, and many a fan thought it a startling omission that 30 years later, neither Ian nor the group had been inducted. Nevertheless, in March 2019, when Roxy Music and Def Leppard were granted recognition, Ian agreed to come and play with Def Leppard for the evening's closing showpiece. The roll call for 'All The Young Dudes' was a star-studded lineup of Def Leppard, Ian, Brian May, Steve Van Zandt, Susanna Hoffs, Phil Manzanera, Rod Argent and Colin Blunstone.

The following month, Mott The Hoople '74' (Ian, Ariel, Morgan and The Rant Band) played eight American dates including Milwaukee, Boston and New York, then crossing the Atlantic for seven British shows – that itinerary including Manchester, Glasgow, Birmingham and London's O2 Shepherd's Bush Empire. Following a return to America from 31 May to 3 June, Ian and The Rant Band played four sold-out shows at City Winery, New York, to mark the milestone of his 80th birthday on the last of the dates.

The list of rock and roll stars who have celebrated such a momentous occasion with a gig, is a small one. Several of those who'd been part of Ian's career or else were closely associated were no longer musically active, and in some cases, not even alive. Shortly after playing with Bad Company on a short British arena tour in October 2016, Mick Ralphs was admitted to hospital after suffering a stroke: putting any ideas of continuing his career in severe jeopardy. In January that year, the music world had mourned the death of David Bowie and also Dale Griffin, the latter having been diagnosed with Alzheimer's, passing away a week later. Among the tributes that poured in was one from Billy Bragg, who was astonished to learn when once invited to record a BBC session, that his producer would be Dale. Billy said Dale was 'a lovely guy to be in the studio with', adding that he always had a soft spot for Mott The Hoople: 'Theirs was the only band I ever really wanted to be a member of, along with Earth, Wind & Fire'.

In January 2017, Overend Watts succumbed to cancer. Ian paid tribute to his former bassist, posting on his website:

My extremely eccentric, lovely mate – Peter Overend Watts – has left the building. Devastated.

In his last years, Overend completed a solo album – provisionally titled *She's Real Gone* – but didn't live to see its release. Angel Air issued it a few months later – its title altered according to Overend's last wishes: *He's Real Gone*.

When Kris Needs interviewed Ian not long afterwards and alluded to his friends' passing, Ian's sadness was evident: 'I was older than all of them by far. Who'd have thought? It's ridiculous'. Steve Hyams – whose obituaries called him a 'former singer and guitarist with Mott The Hoople' (an inaccuracy still found regularly online) – died aged 62 in May 2013, and Nigel Benjamin in August 2019, aged 64. On New Year's Day 2021, Mick Bolton – who toured playing Hammond organ with Mott The Hoople, though he was never an official group member – joined them, aged 72. Several other former Mott members had also experienced major health issues over the years.

In 2019, soon after Ian's 80th birthday, an eleven-date American tour for Mott The Hoople '74 was lined up for October and November, but in September, he suffered a severe attack of tinnitus, something that had previously troubled him though less severely. On medical advice, all further live work had to be cancelled. In February 2020, Ian announced on his website that he would resume touring when the doctors permitted: 'I've no intention of stopping. I just have to find a way around this, and it's difficult. Working on it'. Just how difficult, nobody yet knew. Only days later, the Coronavirus pandemic brought all live work in the performing arts world to a prolonged halt.

Over the years, Ian remained as defiantly unimpressed with new music as he had been in the 1980s, telling Michael Hann in 2018: 'Simon Cowell murdered it. Corporations murdered it in the 1980s'. But a passion for his music, and the way it used to be, still motivated him. Looking back on his old group around the same time, Ian said that every bit of Mott was 'scary, great, annoying, hilarious, triumphant and despondent – everything a band should be'. It had been a slow burn after Mick Ralphs left, and went downhill fast after Mick Ronson joined. Ian believed they could've risen above everything, but it went the opposite way. He felt great when he left, and never regretted it. It was like school for all of them – they learned, had fun learning, and got back together a couple of times.

Though Mott The Hoople only lasted for five years – with several personnel changes – they left an indelible impression on British rock music in the early-1970s, with several classic or near-classic singles and albums that inspired a generation of up-and-coming future names – records that still stand up well, almost half a century later.

Resources

Books
Clayton, D., Smith, T. K., *Heavy Load: Free* (Moonshine, 2000)
Devine, C., *All the Young Dudes: Mott The Hoople and Ian Hunter* (Cherry Red, 1998)
Devine, C., *Rock'n'Roll Sweepstakes: Vol. 1, Mott's Story* (Omnibus, 2019)
Devine, C., *Rock'n'Roll Sweepstakes: Vol. 2, Hunter by Proxy* (Omnibus, 2021)
Garner, K., *The Peel Sessions* (BBC, 2007)
Hunter, I., *Diary of a Rock'n'Roll Star* (Panther, 1974)
Reynolds, S., *Shock and Awe: Glam Rock and its Legacy* (Faber, 2016)
Rosen, S., *Free at Last: The Story of Free and Bad Company* (SAF, 2001)

Articles and Interviews
Chalmers, R., 'Ian Hunter: The truth about Mott The Hoople, the drugs and the manager with a death wish' (Interview) *The Independent*, (23 October 2011)
Davison, P., 'Steve Hyams: Guitarist with Mott The Hoople' (Obituary) *The Independent* (3 June 2013)
Gittins, I., 'Mott The Hoople, Hammersmith Apollo' (Live review) *The Guardian* (2 October 2009)
Hann, M., 'Ian Hunter, rock's great underdog: "Bowie thought I was the head of a motorcycle gang."' *The Guardian* (22 October 2018)
Needs, K., 'Everything Was an Adventure: Ian Hunter' *Record Collector* (December 2018)
Petridis, A., 'Mott The Hoople, O2 Arena' (Live review) *The Guardian* (19 November 2013)
Wall, M., 'Mott The Hoople' *Classic Rock* (October 2009)

Internet
https://www.allmusic.com AllMusic
www.discogs.com Discogs
www.45cat.com 45cat vinyl database
www.hunter-mott.com Mott The Hoople, Ian Hunter website
www.justabuzz.com Just a Buzz – A Mott The Hoople fansite